A Handbook for Classroom MANAGEMENT that Works

Robert J. Marzano

Barbara B. Gaddy

Maria C. Foseid

Mark P. Foseid

Jana S. Marzano

Association for Supervision and Curriculum Development
Alexandria, Virginia USA

Association for Supervision and Curriculum Development
1703 N. Beauregard St. • Alexandria, VA 22311-1714 USA
Phone: 800-933-2723 or 703-578-9600 • Fax: 703-575-5400
Web site: www.ascd.org • E-mail: member@ascd.org
Author guidelines: www.ascd.org/write

Gene R. Carter, *Executive Director;* Nancy Modrak, *Director of Publishing;* Julie Houtz, *Director of Book Editing & Production;* Tim Sniffin and Katie Martin, *Project Managers;* Shelley Prince, Senior Graphic Designer; Cynthia Stock, *Typesetter;* Dina Murray Seamon, *Production Specialist*

All Web links in this book are correct as of the publication date below but may have become inactive or otherwise modified since that time. If you notice a deactivated or changed link, please e-mail books@ascd.org with the words "Link Update" in the subject line. In your message, please specify the Web link, the book title, and the page number on which the link appears.

PAPERBACK ISBN-13: 978-1-4166-0236-1 • ASCD product #105012   s11/05
PAPERBACK ISBN-10: 1-4166-0236-4
e-book editions: retail PDF ISBN-13: 978-1-4166-0362-7; retail PDF ISBN-10: 1-4166-0362-X •
netLibrary ISBN-13: 978-1-4166-0360-3; netLibrary ISBN-10: 1-4166-0360-3 •
ebrary ISBN-13: 978-1-4166-0361-0; ebrary ISBN-10: 1-4166-0361-1

Also available as an e-book through ebrary, netLibrary, and many online booksellers (see Books in Print for the ISBNs).

Quantity discounts for the paperback book: 10–49 copies, 10%; 50+ copies, 15%; for 500 or more copies, call 800-933-2723, ext. 5634, or 703-575-5634.

Library of Congress Cataloging-in-Publication Data
A handbook for classroom management that works / Robert J. Marzano . . . [et al.].
    p. cm.
  Includes bibliographical references and index.
  ISBN 1-4166-0236-4 (alk. paper)
  1. Classroom management. I. Marzano, Robert J. II. Association for Supervision and Curriculum Development.

  LB3013.H36 2005
  371.102'4—dc22

                                                                    2005024849

12 11 10 09 08 07   12 11 10 9 8 7 6 5 4 3 2

A Handbook for Classroom Management that Works

INTRODUCTION

Today's educators have more research to guide classroom practice than ever before in the history of education in the United States. Much of the research regarding classroom management has been synthesized and described in the book *Classroom Management That Works: Research-Based Strategies for Every Teacher* (Marzano, 2003). Based on an analysis of more than 100 studies on classroom management, the book identified seven research-based elements of effective classroom management:

- Rules and procedures
- Discipline and consequences
- Teacher-student relationships
- Mental set
- Student responsibility
- Getting off to a good start
- Management at the school level

This handbook is intended as a self-study guide to effective strategies in each of these areas. Although you can use this handbook without having read *Classroom Management That Works*, we recommend that you do read it because it establishes the research base for the recommendations in the handbook.

How the Handbook Is Organized

This handbook is organized into seven sections corresponding to the seven elements of effective classroom management. Each section follows the same format. A brief introduction describes the topics addressed within the section and their relationship to classroom management. These introductions

1

include a set of questions titled "Reflecting on Your Current Beliefs and Practices" that ask you to think about what you do and the assumptions from which you operate for each of the seven elements of effective classroom management.

The heart of each section is a set of modules with specific strategies and suggestions for classroom practice. These strategies and suggestions address all grade levels and provide a comprehensive treatment of effective classroom management.

Finally, each section ends with a two-part "Section Reflection." The first part, "Checking Your Understanding," poses questions or hypothetical situations. The intent is to give you an opportunity to determine whether you understand what has been presented in the modules and to help you apply what you have learned. The second part, "A Self-Assessment," is a series of questions to help you determine how effectively you use the strategies and suggestions presented in the modules.

How to Use the Handbook

You can use this handbook as a tool for self-study by working through the seven sections and the modules at your own pace. By reflecting on your current beliefs and practices, reading the strategies and suggestions in the modules, checking your understanding of the information presented, and then assessing yourself, you can gain new insights into the art and science of classroom management. If you use the handbook for self-study, you can also choose the sequence in which you will address the seven sections. You can read them in the order presented or in an order that suits your level of curiosity about each section.

Another approach is to use this handbook within the context of a study team. Many schools emphasize the importance of staff members becoming a "community of learners." Study teams are one of the best ways to accomplish this goal. The basic purpose of a study team is to examine a topic in depth as a group of committed professionals. The team should meet at least once every two weeks for at least an hour. Before each meeting, each study team member reads the same section of the handbook. For example, let's assume that each study team member has read the section on "Student Responsibility." When the team meets, each member would share his or her responses to the questions in the opening reflection set, titled "Thinking About Your Current Beliefs and Practices." This sharing would help the group members understand one another's perspectives on student responsibility for classroom management. Study team members might also share their responses to the questions in the "Checking Your Understanding" lists and "Self-Assessments." Next, study team members would identify and discuss the practices and strategies mentioned in the modules that they found particularly interesting. They might comment on their personal experiences with selected strategies and suggestions or explain their adaptations of them. They might also identify questions they have about the strategies and suggestions in the modules.

Using this approach, study team members simply discuss their reactions to and experiences with the strategies and suggestions in the modules. At a much more active and energetic level, study team members might try out selected strategies or suggestions between team meetings. A team member trying out a particular strategy might collect some informal data on its effectiveness. These data might be as simple as observing the behavior of students during and after use of the strategy. The team member would then share these data with colleagues during the next study team meeting. In this way, the study team could carry out focused action research projects on selected strategies and suggestions.

A Commitment to Self-Discovery and Excellence

Whatever approach you take, it is important to use this handbook as a tool for your personal development as a classroom educator. Regardless of your level of experience in the classroom, this handbook will provide some new ideas and perspectives on classroom management. A willingness to consider and even try out new ideas and perspectives is the ultimate test of an educator's commitment to self-discovery and excellence. We hope that this handbook is a useful tool in helping you realize that commitment.

RULES AND PROCEDURES

Perhaps the most obvious aspect of effective classroom management is classroom rules and procedures. Rules and procedures convey the message that "I'm here to teach and you're here to learn." They give students the structure they need and also help them feel that the classroom is a safe and predictable place.

In this handbook, we use the terms *rules* and *procedures*. Both refer to stated expectations about students' behavior, but the terms differ in important ways. A *rule* identifies general expectations or standards; a single rule can encompass a wide range of expected behaviors. A *procedure* communicates expectations for specific behaviors. Effective teachers use both rules and procedures. For example, you might establish the *rule* "Respect other students and their property" and also create separate *procedures* for returning books to the appropriate place in the classroom and participating respectfully in class discussions.

The number and kind of rules and procedures vary from class to class and from grade to grade, but every good teacher has them. How students treat one another, when and how students may leave the room, and when it is appropriate to speak out in class are common topics for rules and procedures in every grade.

A theme that runs through this section is the importance of considering when and how to involve students in establishing rules and procedures. Research clearly supports the notion that designing and implementing rules and procedures in class, and even at home, significantly influences students' behavior and learning. But research also indicates that rules and procedures should not simply be imposed *on* students; they should be created *with* students. Effective teachers take the time to explain the reasons behind particular rules and procedures, involve students in creating them, and seek their input as much as appropriate. When students are involved in this process, they are more likely to make classroom rules and procedures their own.

This section highlights six areas to consider for classroom rules and procedures:

- Module 1: General Classroom Behavior
- Module 2: Beginning and Ending the Period or the Day
- Module 3: Transitions and Interruptions
- Module 4: Use of Materials and Equipment
- Module 5: Group Work
- Module 6: Seat Work and Teacher-Led Activities

A word of caution: It is counterproductive to set rules and procedures in all of these areas. Inundating students with rules and procedures for every aspect of the classroom clearly is not a good idea. Rules, particularly for young students, should be few—for most grades, no more than eight. In addition, rules should be worded succinctly, making them easier for students to recall and therefore follow.

Each of these modules offers strategies, examples, and practical suggestions for putting these ideas into practice, as well as opportunities for you to reflect on your use of the guidance provided. We encourage you to use the suggestions offered here—along with *Classroom Management That Works* and other resources—to set appropriate rules and procedures for your classroom and your unique group of students.

■ Reflecting on Your Current Beliefs and Practices

Before reading the modules in this section, take some time to reflect on your beliefs, perspectives, and current practices regarding rules and procedures for the classroom. Then write your answers to the following questions in the space provided. Your responses will give you a basis for comparison as you read about the strategies recommended in these modules.

• What kinds of rules and procedures do you typically set for your classroom?

• What are some of the reasons for setting classroom rules and procedures?

• How might classroom rules and procedures differ from the elementary to the secondary level?

• Should students be involved in establishing rules and procedures? If so, how?

- Setting rules and procedures is not usually a process that students think of as fun. What are some creative, interesting ways to engage them in the process?

- Think of a time when a classroom seemed to be well managed. What general rules or expectations for behavior did students seem to be following?

- Creating a classroom with no rules or one with too many highly specific rules can lead to problems. What are your thoughts about how to create the right balance?

- Posting lists in a visible place in the classroom is one way to help students remember classroom rules and procedures. What are some other ways?

General Classroom Behavior

In nearly every situation in life, spoken and unspoken rules guide how we interact with and treat other people. As friends and colleagues, for example, we expect consideration and respect from one another. As neighbors we share expectations about such things as noise and how and where we park our cars. Generally we try to observe other rules of common courtesy.

In many situations, the societal rules for our interactions with one another are unspoken. For example, most movie theaters don't have a posted list of rules for waiting in line, but the unspoken rules are clear: After you buy your ticket, go to the end of the line of people waiting to get into the theater; don't cut in line even if you see someone you know; and don't shove or push to get into the theater. Whether spoken or unspoken, one easy way to think about overall expectations for behavior is the golden rule: Do unto others as you would have them do unto you.

Rules and procedures for general classroom behavior deal with the broad areas of respect and courtesy as well as more specific issues, such as listening to the teacher or to classmates who are speaking, and being in the assigned seat when class begins. In some classrooms, teachers involve students in establishing overall class rules for conduct. Involving students helps to build their buy-in and responsibility for the overall environment of the classroom.

Recommendations for Classroom Practice

Establishing rules and shared expectations for general conduct helps to lay a solid foundation for effective classroom management. In this module, we discuss the following specific strategies:

- Writing a class pledge or promise
- Establishing overall classroom rules and procedures
- Consistently reinforcing norms

Regardless of the set of rules or expectations developed, it's important to post them in a visible place in the classroom—for example, on the classroom door, on the wall near the clock, or on a cabinet door. These reminders, which students can easily refer to throughout the day, help students adhere to shared rules.

Writing a Class Pledge or Promise

Many effective teachers involve students in writing a class pledge or promise. This strategy helps create a shared sense of responsibility for the classroom, respect for self and others, and an overall culture of learning. It also is a great way to reinforce students' responsibility for the management of the classroom, as the examples in Figure 1.1 illustrate. Asking students to sign the pledge further reinforces student buy-in and responsibility. A class promise can also be

Figure 1.1
Class Promise and Pledge

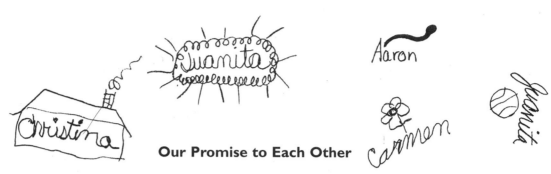

Our Promise to Each Other

When we care about each other in our classroom, we share what we have, listen carefully, help each other learn, work hard, and have fun together. We understand that everyone makes mistakes, that we stand up for ourselves and others, and that when someone asks us to stop, we stop. This is who we are even when no one is watching.

My School Pledge

I pledge today to do my best
In reading, math, and all of the rest.
I promise to obey the rules
In my class and in my school.
I'll respect myself and others, too.
I'll expect the best in all I do.
I am here to learn all I can,
To try my best and be all I am.

communicated in other forms—for example, through a poem such as that in Figure 1.2.

Establishing Overall Classroom Rules and Procedures

In addition to—or in place of—a class pledge or promise, some teachers establish a few briefly worded rules for general classroom behavior. In general, classroom rules, such as those in Figure 1.3, deal with respect, politeness, and consideration, but other general rules also help keep the classroom safe and more conducive to learning.

Many teachers engage their students in establishing overall classroom rules and procedures. For example, you might facilitate a discussion at the beginning of the year about when it is appropriate and not appropriate for students to leave their seats, emphasizing the importance of demonstrating politeness and respect for others. Such a discussion typically involves identifying expected behaviors and procedures for using the pencil sharpener, getting resources and materials from central places in the room, returning materials to shelves, and conferring with other students sitting across the room.

Although there are, of course, some common overall rules that elementary and secondary teachers should establish, rules also vary depending on the age and grade level of students. For example, many elementary school teachers assign specific seats for their students at the beginning of the year. At the secondary level, however, teachers frequently let students sit where they choose as long as their seating choice does not interfere with their learning. Allowing students to choose their own place in the classroom is a sign of respect for their maturity. Students also appreciate this approach, which helps build their support for rules and procedures set by the teacher.

In addition to general rules for classroom behavior, some teachers create graphics or posters that emphasize the importance of character or specific personal characteristics, such as honesty, integrity, or respect, as shown in Figure 1.4.

Figure 1.2

Classroom Poem

A Circle of Friends

We've joined together as classmates as the new year begins.
A year full of learning while we become friends.
We'll share and be kind as we work and we play.
Our friendship will grow with each passing day.

Figure 1.3

Overall Classroom Rules

Classroom Rules (1st Grade)

1. Be safe.
2. Be kind.
3. Be polite.

Classroom Rules (2nd Grade)

1. Listen carefully.
2. Follow directions.
3. Work quietly. Do not disturb others who are working.
4. Respect others. Be kind with your words and actions.
5. Respect school and personal property.
6. Work and play safely.

Classroom Rules (3rd Grade)

1. Be kind and respectful to others and yourself.
2. Listen when others are speaking.
3. Use your manners and be safe.
4. Keep your hands and mean words to yourself.
5. Have fun.

Our Basic Rights

1. All students have the right to be treated with respect.
2. All teachers have the right to be treated with respect.
3. Everyone has the right to feel safe in the teaching and learning environment.
4. Everyone must demonstrate a respect for the school's property.

Rules for Classroom Behavior (Secondary)

1. Respect one another at all times.
2. Maintain eye contact when communicating with others or when someone—a teacher or a classmate—is speaking.
3. Use "6-inch voices" when working in small groups or in pairs.
4. When working in groups, say "please" and "thank you"; praise each other and use good manners.
5. Remember: Only one person speaks at a time.

Making Our Classroom a Place for Learning

1. Respect others—when someone is speaking, listen.
2. Follow directions.
3. Keep hands, feet, objects, and unkind remarks to yourself.
4. Bring required materials to class.
5. Be in your seat when the bell rings.
6. Raise your hand.
7. Remember the rules we set for leaving your seat or leaving the classroom: Maintain respect and quiet, think before you act, and minimize disruptions to the learning process.

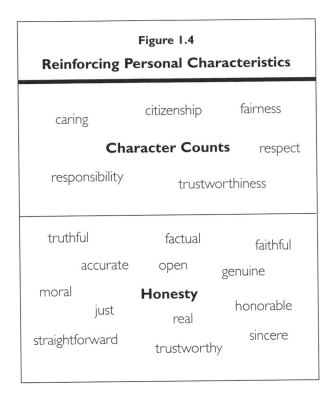

Figure 1.4
Reinforcing Personal Characteristics

caring   citizenship   fairness

Character Counts   respect

responsibility   trustworthiness

truthful   factual   faithful

accurate   open   genuine

moral   **Honesty**   honorable

just   real

straightforward   sincere

trustworthy

the room; teachers encourage quiet by being the first to raise their hands, stop talking, and turn their attention to the principal. Students learn to notice that adults' hands are raised, and then they stop talking and put their hands up, too. Used consistently, this approach catches on and the room becomes quiet more quickly. This technique is a respectful way to bring a large group to order without raising voices.

In addition to broad rules for conduct, many teachers also set rules for more specific behaviors, such as listening, or for bully-proofing the classroom. As with other rules, you should post these in a visible place in the classroom and consider adding symbols or drawings to make them easier for students to remember, as shown in Figures 1.5 and 1.6.

For general classroom procedures, you can establish simple gestures or symbols to communicate basic messages in the classroom. Here are some examples:

- *Raised hand.* Raise your hand to signal that it's time to be quiet and pay attention. Students raise their hands as they stop talking and look at you.
- *Hands over ears.* Put your hands over your ears to signal that group work has become too noisy, or quietly walk over and flick the overhead lights on and off.
- *Raised book or pencil.* A student holds up a book or a pencil to signal that he needs help—for example, during study time.

One common situation in which the raised-hand technique can be used is the school assembly. The principal raises her hand to quiet

Figure 1.5
Rules for Listening

1. Eyes on speaker.
2. Mouth quiet.
3. Be still.
4. Hands free.
5. Listen.

Figure 1.6

Bully-Proofing Rules

1. We will not bully other students.
2. We will help others who are being bullied by speaking out and by getting adult help.
3. We will use extra effort to include all students in activities at our school.

Here's another way to think about it: **HA HA SO!**

H = *Help others.* If someone is being bullied, step in and help!

A = *Assert yourself.* Speak up or walk away.

H = *Humor helps.* Maintain a good sense of humor and keep the situation light!

A = *Avoid.* Stay away from negative situations.

S = *Self-talk.* Keep your own internal "talk" positive about what happened. Don't blame yourself for something you didn't do.

O = *Own it.* At the same time, take responsibility for your own actions.

Consistently Reinforcing Norms

Regardless of the specific rules or procedures established for general classroom behavior, it's important to follow through consistently and to reinforce these norms. You can do this in a variety of ways. Here are some specific suggestions:

• Model the procedures for students, or ask students to participate in modeling.

• Provide time for students to talk or write about why rules and procedures for general classroom behavior might be important and useful.

• Provide feedback to students about the extent to which they are following the rules and procedures so they can refine, improve, or correct their behavior.

Beginning and Ending the Period or the Day

One way to get the most instructional time out of the day or class period is to establish rules and procedures for how you begin and end your time with students. Beginning and ending well—and consistently—sets the tone for the classroom and helps students know what to expect. It is one way that you can reinforce a sense of structure and consistency and communicate that the classroom is a place for learning.

Recommendations for Classroom Practice

Like other rules and procedures, the specific ways in which teachers start and end the day or period vary. Regardless of the specific routines established, however, whether at an elementary school, middle school, or high school, classroom management is enhanced when teachers establish routines that communicate *order* and *learning* at the same time. In particular, we recommend the following strategies:

- Beginning with a balance of learning and "administrivia"
- Establishing shared activities that reinforce class unity
- Ending with activities that reinforce learning and discipline

Beginning with a Balance of Learning and "Administrivia"

It's easy to fall into the habit of spending the first part of class simply taking attendance, passing out completed assignments, and dealing with other administrative tasks, often referred to as "administrivia." Obviously, determining who is present and who is absent is important, but to make the most of students' learning time—and your own time—you might start the day by giving students an opportunity to set their own learning goals for the day based on overall goals you have established. As we note in Section 3, "Teacher-Student Relationships," this approach also conveys the idea that you care about your students' interests and personal goals.

Many effective teachers also give students "sponge" activities to work on—sometimes referred to as the "daily starter" or "daily warm-up"—when they enter the classroom. Madeline Hunter is frequently credited with the idea of using these activities to minimize gaps in students' learning—to "soak up" every available minute of learning time. Many sponge activities are designed to help students review their prior learning or activate background knowledge as they learn something new.

Many online and print resources provide ideas for sponge activities. Depending on students' grade level and the content area being studied, you might start the day with journal writing, puzzles, math problems, brain teasers, or brainstorming activities. The sponge activities are as varied as teachers themselves. However, the activities must be meaningful and tied to specific learning goals for students. In addition to, or in place of, sponge activities, you might ask students to talk quietly in pairs or in small groups about the previous day's homework assignment and what they learned.

Establishing Shared Activities That Reinforce Class Unity

Many teachers, particularly teachers of elementary students, begin the day with activities that establish and reinforce a sense of community and unity among students. Students who feel that they are part of a community of learners, who have the experience of "being in this together," are more likely to be part of the solution than the problem.

One way to start the day is to acknowledge birthdays or other important events in students' lives, or to recite the Pledge of Allegiance or the school pledge. This might also be the time to recognize particular achievements of the class as a whole or to announce class activities, such as a family potluck or an upcoming schoolwide science fair. Figure 2.1 summarizes how an elementary school teacher might start the day.

Ending with Activities That Reinforce Learning and Discipline

Like activities for beginning the day or the class period, ending activities—when used

---

Figure 2.1
Starting the Day: An Example

- The teacher greets each student individually at the door.

- Students read silently for a short time while the teacher quickly takes attendance and then stops by each student's desk to provide feedback about individual behavior or academic performance.

- The entire class stands and recites the Pledge of Allegiance and then listens to a recording of "God Bless America."

- The teacher verbally recognizes students as a class and lets them know they are welcomed and cared for.

---

consistently—help establish the classroom as a predictable environment for learning. There are a variety of ways to end the day or period, such as homework assignments, answering questions, reflecting on learning, or reminding students about putting away supplies. Teachers of young students, in particular, can use the time to reinforce good habits, such as cleaning up after oneself and storing materials in their proper place. Teachers also frequently use this time to review homework assignments. To reinforce good study habits, you might create a list of brief homework reminders or guidelines, such as those shown in Figure 2.2, and refer students to these at the end of the day or class period.

Figure 2.2

End-of-Class Homework Reminders

- Plan a daily homework time.
- Take home everything you'll need.
- Choose a quiet study place.
- Read and follow all directions.
- Do your work neatly and carefully.
- Ask for help if you need it, but do the work yourself.
- Keep your homework in a special place.
- Return your homework on time.

Secondary teachers often use the end-of-class time to bring closure to the day's learning process. One common approach is to ask students to do a reflection writing activity (in a journal, for example) about what they learned that day, then pair up and share what they wrote. One way to extend this process is to ask the pair to write key points they learned that day on a note card and turn it in to you. Students also might jot down questions or short notes about things they found confusing or unclear, or something they would like to learn about in more depth.

Transitions and Interruptions

Leaving the classroom for lunch. Using the restroom. Going to the library, computer center, or resource room. Moving from one class to another or from one learning center to another. Going outside for recess. The list of things that can and do interrupt time for learning is long. Regardless of the grade level, every teacher needs to deal with certain interruptions and transitions—both within the classroom and from the classroom to other areas of the school or school grounds.

For students who have difficulty focusing, such interruptions can be especially distracting and translate into even less learning time if not managed well. Because many students appear to have difficulties with attention and focus, the need to effectively manage interruptions is pressing.

Recommendations for Classroom Practice

Establishing rules and procedures for transitions and interruptions is an important aspect of classroom management. Specifically, we suggest the following strategies:

- Establishing rules and procedures for recurring situations
- Practicing transitions and potential interruptions
- Engaging students as leaders during transitions and interruptions

Establishing Rules and Procedures for Recurring Situations

A useful strategy for transitions and interruptions is to establish rules and procedures for recurring situations, such as completing one classroom activity and beginning another, using the bathroom, and leaving the classroom for lunch. By creating rules and procedures, sharing these with students, making sure they understand them, and asking for their feedback (when appropriate), you can prevent unnecessary delays and problems.

The complexity and type of rules or procedures established vary greatly, depending on students' age and maturity. In some situations, the rules students must follow might be very specific, such as the bathroom rules listed in Figure 3.1 for an elementary-level class. Similarly, you may find that students need a great deal of structure when moving from one learning center to the next. Figure 3.2 is an example of how one elementary-level teacher facilitates this process.

Rules and procedures can be very simple and straightforward—perhaps as simple as a particular comment you make or a signal you give just before a break in the learning process. For example, you might say, "Please take the next five minutes to complete the project you are working on" or quietly write on the board "Five minutes left." Of course, in the latter

---

Figure 3.1

Bathroom Rules

1. No talking in the bathroom.
2. You have only three minutes for bathroom time.
3. Do your job and don't mess around.
4. Go to the bathroom only during group bathroom breaks, recess, or independent work time.

We promise to follow the bathroom rules. *(Each student in the class signs the list.)*

Figure 3.2

Moving from One Learning Center to Another

Teacher: "Okay, everyone, you have two minutes to finish your work." *(The teacher gives students two minutes.)*

Teacher: "Now please clean up your center." *(The teacher provides time.)*

Teacher: "Okay. Now we will find out which center to go to next." *(The teacher points to the chart that lists students by name and by center.)*

The teacher then leads the class in the song "Open and Shut Them" as a cue for attention, and students begin to move to their new centers.

---

situation, you must have established this as a routine so students know to periodically look at the board as they are working.

Practicing Transitions and Potential Interruptions

When the bell rings (or you signal that it's time to move to another activity or go to recess), mayhem is much more likely to ensue if a procedure has not become routine for students. One way to ensure that students automatically know and recall what to do is to give them opportunities to practice routines and to take time to reinforce expected behaviors. In fact, the point of fire and disaster drills is to make routines automatic, which is critically important if a true disaster situation were to arise.

The same can be said for other, less urgent situations. One effective strategy, particularly at the beginning of the year, is to role-play various situations. Role playing engages students in practicing and demonstrating behavior that works—as well as behavior that doesn't work. This can be a useful process for many things that occur in the classroom, from tardiness to unexpected classroom visitors.

One secondary teacher, for example, asks students to practice being in their seats *before* the bell rings to work on the sponge activity written on the board. Students practice what it means to create a "businesslike atmosphere" at the beginning and end of class. They also practice what to do and how to act if they arrive late to class.

One routine this teacher has established is that the tardy student comes into the room quietly and picks up a "tardy pass" from a basket near the door. The student completes the pass—filling in his or her name, the date, and any reason for or comment about being late—and gives it to the teacher. The teacher deals with any resulting consequences on an individual basis, depending on the student's reason for being tardy.

Role playing these types of situations can be effective but also lighthearted. For example, in addition to asking students to practice positive, workable behaviors when arriving to class, this teacher asks a student to volunteer to demonstrate arriving in a way that does *not* help create a useful learning environment. The volunteer student typically dashes into the classroom, laughing and talking loudly, tosses his or her books on the desk (some of which fall to the floor), and immediately tries to distract other students from whatever they're doing. Talking about how to act and how not to act is useful, but seeing the behaviors in action makes them more real.

Engaging Students as Leaders During Transitions and Interruptions

One way to ease transition times and build student buy-in is to have students take leadership roles. For example, you might assign a student—or ask for a student to volunteer—to serve as the line leader as the class lines up to go to recess, walks quietly down the hall, and walks outside to the playground. Another student might be the class leader for lunch breaks. Students also might serve in other roles, such as classroom greeter for expected visitors; in this case, the student would quietly meet the visitor at the classroom door, welcome him or her, and show the visitor to an appropriate seat. Student leadership roles such as these can be rotated from day to day or week to week to give more students an opportunity to share responsibility for the management of the classroom. A chart like the one shown in Figure 3.3 can help reinforce daily leadership roles.

Figure 3.3
Students as Leaders

Help Wanted!
(Place student's name or picture in each cell.)

	Recess Line Leader	Lunch Leader	Leader of the Pledge	Technology Director	Mail Deliverer
Monday					
Tuesday					
Wednesday					
Thursday					
Friday					

Use of Materials and Equipment

Another possible area for rules and procedures is the use of materials and equipment, such as books, desks, and storage areas, as well as the care and handling of specialty materials and equipment. Rules and procedures for appropriately using classroom materials and equipment lay the groundwork for students' responsible use of shared resources as they become adults.

Recommendations for Classroom Practice

Regardless of students' age or the type of classroom, we recommend the following strategies:

• Establishing rules and procedures for common classroom materials and equipment
• Establishing rules and procedures for specialty materials and equipment

Establishing Rules and Procedures for Common Classroom Materials and Equipment

Although classrooms across the United States have a variety of materials, a few staples of K–12 education have been in use for countless years: pencils or pens, textbooks and other books, paper, desks or tables, pencil sharpeners, and staplers, to name a few. Many teachers set a few simple and direct rules for handling common classroom materials and equipment, such

as "Treat the things we share with care" and "Keep common areas clean and neat." At both the elementary and secondary levels, it is a good idea to have rules and procedures for how books and resources are distributed, stored, and collected and for how students take care of their own desks. Depending on students' age and maturity, you also might set rules and procedures related to your own desk and storage areas and the use of the drinking fountain, sink, pencil sharpener, and other general classroom equipment.

Many teachers also set a few simple rules for materials that students should bring to class each day. Figure 4.1 shows some basic expectations that you might establish—with or without students' input, depending on grade level, maturity, and your preference.

Figure 4.1 also shows an example of "borrowing rules" that you might establish for borrowing common materials from a friend or from a community "borrowing shelf." One easy way to collect materials for this area, especially at the end of the school year, is to gather up pencils, pens, blank notebooks, paper, paper clips, and other supplies that students leave in the halls or in class throughout the year (and that don't clearly belong to a particular student). You can keep these materials, which students may borrow if they forget to bring

---

Figure 4.1

Rules for Common Materials and Supplies

Be Prepared Every Day

- Bring a pencil or pen to class.

- Bring a spiral notebook for note taking and other work.

- Bring your textbook to class each day.

- If you forget your materials, remember the Borrowing Rules we set:

   – Try to borrow what you need from a classmate. OR . . .

   – You may borrow up to five times from the community shelf.

   – Put a checkmark next to your name each time you borrow something.

   – Don't forget to return what you have borrowed at the end of class.

---

something to class, in a community box or drawer or on a shelf.

The advantage of this approach is that it supports the learning process and, at the secondary level, is one less reason for students to go to their lockers during the day. The disadvantage is that students may forget to return the materials they borrowed.

Establishing Rules and Procedures for Specialty Materials and Equipment

Most classrooms have materials and equipment that require special or careful handling. For example, many classrooms have one or more computers, software, and perhaps a printer; others have maps, globes, scales, and other specialty equipment; and art and science classes are filled with special supplies and tools.

Given the diverse array of classroom resources and equipment, this section does not include detailed suggestions for rules and procedures regarding the handling and storage of specific items. You yourself must identify the items that need special handling, set appropriate rules, and ensure that students understand them. For very young children, the appropriate rule might simply be "Do not touch." As students mature, however, you might gradually give them expanded responsibilities regarding specialty equipment.

Regardless of students' age, however, every teacher must stress "safety first." In fact, ensuring that students understand safety procedures should be the first order of business at the beginning of the school year. This can be as straightforward as establishing a rule for young students that they may use scissors only while seated and then being vigilant about enforcing this rule. For other materials and equipment, such as chemicals or specialized art equipment, more detailed rules and procedures may be in order.

Setting rules and procedures in this area is important not only for building students'

responsibility overall but for ensuring that equipment and specialty materials last a long time. As with most areas dealing with classroom management, you might ask students to help establish rules and procedures for the use of materials and equipment and thereby build students' leadership skills.

Group Work

Cooperative learning and other group activities can be effective classroom instructional strategies, not only academically but also as ways to develop students' relationships with one another. By working with their peers, students can learn to express themselves clearly, to listen, to compromise, to value others, and to take leadership roles. For group work to be most useful, however, teachers should establish a foundation of rules and procedures and reinforce them throughout the year.

Recommendations for Classroom Practice

Setting and reinforcing expectations for group work can greatly contribute to a better managed classroom. In particular, we recommend the following strategies:

- Establishing rules and procedures for moving into and out of groups
- Setting expectations for group behavior and focus

Establishing Rules and Procedures for Moving into and out of Groups

Successful teachers know the value, particularly at the elementary level, of establishing straightforward cues or procedures for students moving into—and out of—groups in the classroom. One kindergarten teacher, for example, signals that it's time for students to move from table work to group seating by saying, "Let's have the quietest table move to group seating first." She then selects a table to move. While students are moving, often they have not pushed their chairs in, so she might say, "Oops. Who forgot to push their chairs in?" Some students go back to push in their chairs, and she resumes table selections after the first group is completely seated.

A 5th grade teacher uses the phrase "wait for the magic word," which signals to students that it's time to pay particular attention. When he says the magic word, students move. Other teachers might use a simple word such as "go," but he makes it a bit more fun by using "spaghetti" as the magic word. Students also have learned that students in the first group that's ready and on task get a free point. During the week, students accumulate points; those with the most points by Wednesday of each week get to play the classroom game (for example, Bingo) that day during free time.

Regardless of the particular cue or signal you use, make sure it's clear to students which group they will be working in and where they will be seated. You might put a list of preassigned groups on an overhead image or post it on the wall.

General classroom seating arrangements also can support the process of group work. One teacher, for example, seats students in pairs in four rows, each row beginning at the front of the room and ending in the back. To illustrate, assume each row comprises four pairs of students. Students can work individually, "pair share," or form small groups of four without having to get up and rearrange their seats. The advantage to this approach is that it minimizes classroom disruption; the teacher also can easily monitor and maintain groups by weaving between the rows.

Setting Expectations for Group Behavior and Focus

Another area worth attending to is expectations for how students will interact as they work together. These expectations can be written specifically for group work, like those in Figure 5.1, or more broadly to address how students treat one another in the classroom. Either way, developing a few straightforward guidelines helps create a culture of mutual respect.

High school or upper middle school teachers, in particular, might also write objectives for behavior and then give students feedback about behavior when they provide feedback on academic objectives. For example, a teacher and a student might determine that the student needs support during group work in dealing with students who express differing opinions. In this case, together the teacher and the student might set the behavioral objective "Listens when others are sharing ideas and opinions."

Another option is to develop self-assessment forms that students can use to evaluate their own behavior in various learning formats. For

---

Figure 5.1

Expectations for Group Behavior

Problem Solvers Are Able To . . .

- Listen
- Apologize
- Compromise and cooperate
- Offer to share now or share later
- Avoid arguments
- Forgive, forget, and move on
- Show that they care about others' feelings
- Stay calm

Be a problem solver!

Cooperative Group Rules

1. Take turns talking quietly.
2. Listen to each other's ideas.
3. Praise each other's ideas.
4. Help each other when asked.
5. Stay together until everyone is finished.
6. Talk about how you worked well together and how you might improve.

---

example, if the learning format is direct instruction, students might rate themselves on particular behavioral objectives using the self-assessment scale shown in Figure 5.2. If the learning format is working with a partner, students might use the self-assessment scale shown in Figure 5.3. Figures 5.4 and 5.5, respectively, include behavioral objectives and

Figure 5.2
Behavioral Objectives and Student Self-Assessment for Direct Instruction

Behavioral Objectives

1. Maintain eye contact with the person speaking (a classmate or the teacher).

2. Raise your hand when you wish to ask a question or make a comment.

3. Be open-minded about comments and questions from peers.

4. Stay focused on the learning activity. If you have thoughts that are not related to the learning activity, notice them, but then put them aside until the class period is over. (This behavior is known as *bracketing*.)

Self-Assessment

Rate your performance on the behavioral objectives. Note that the scale ranges from 1 (not there yet) to 4 (I behaved at top performance). Briefly describe why you think the rating is an accurate assessment of your behavior. Then discuss your self-assessment with your teacher.

1	2	3	4
Not there yet			I behaved at top performance

1. Maintain eye contact with the person speaking (a classmate or the teacher).

Rating _____

Reason(s) _____

_____

2. Raise your hand when you wish to ask a question or make a comment.

Rating _____

Reason(s) _____

_____

3. Be open-minded about comments and questions from peers.

Rating _____

Reason(s) _____

_____

4. Stay focused on the learning activity. If you have thoughts that are not related to the learning activity, notice them, but then put them aside until the class period is over.

Rating _____

Reason(s) _____

_____

Figure 5.3

Behavioral Objectives and Student Self-Assessment for Working with a Partner

---

Behavioral Objectives

1. Stay on task.

2. Use 6-inch voices.

3. Make sure that everyone participates. One person should not dominate the conversation or take charge of completing the task on his or her own.

4. Respect and encourage one another's ideas and contributions.

Self-Assessment

Rate your performance on the behavioral objectives. Note that the scale ranges from 1 (not there yet) to 4 (I behaved at top performance). Briefly describe why you think the rating is an accurate assessment of your behavior. Then discuss your self-assessment with your teacher.

1	2	3	4
Not there yet			I behaved at top performance

1. Stay on task.

Rating _____

Reason(s) _____

_____

2. Use 6-inch voices.

Rating _____

Reason(s) _____

_____

3. Make sure that everyone participates. One person should not dominate the conversation or take charge of completing the task on his or her own.

Rating _____

Reason(s) _____

_____

4. Respect and encourage one another's ideas and contributions.

Rating _____

Reason(s) _____

_____

Figure 5.4

Behavioral Objectives and Student Self-Assessment for Working in Groups

Behavioral Objectives

1. Stay on task.
2. Use a quiet voice.
3. If group roles have been assigned, support one another in your assigned roles. For example, assist the leader, timekeeper, recorder, and reporter by cooperating and participating in the group task.
4. Be open-minded.
5. Participate in the group's activities and assignments.

Self-Assessment

Rate your performance on the behavioral objectives. Note that the scale ranges from 1 (not there yet) to 4 (I behaved at top performance). Briefly describe why you think the rating is an accurate assessment of your behavior. Then discuss your self-assessment with your teacher.

1	2	3	4
Not there yet			I behaved at top performance

1. Stay on task.
Rating _____
Reason(s) _____
_____

2. Use a quiet voice.
Rating _____
Reason(s) _____
_____

3. If group roles have been assigned, support one another in your assigned roles.
Rating _____
Reason(s) _____
_____

4. Be open-minded.
Rating _____
Reason(s) _____
_____

5. Participate in the group's activities and assignments.
Rating _____
Reason(s) _____
_____

Figure 5.5

Behavioral Objectives and Student Self-Assessment for Working Individually

---

Behavioral Objectives

1. Raise hand to get permission to talk with teacher or classmates.
2. Contribute to a quiet atmosphere for learning.
3. Maintain focus on the task at hand.
4. Avoid side conversations.

Self-Assessment

Rate your performance on the behavioral objectives. Note that the scale ranges from 1 (not there yet) to 4 (I behaved at top performance). Briefly describe why you think the rating is an accurate assessment of your behavior. Then discuss your self-assessment with your teacher.

1	2	3	4
Not there yet			I behaved at top performance

1. Raise hand to get permission to talk with teacher or classmates.

Rating _____

Reason(s) _____

_____

2. Contribute to a quiet atmosphere for learning.

Rating _____

Reason(s) _____

_____

3. Maintain focus on the task at hand.

Rating _____

Reason(s) _____

_____

4. Avoid side conversations.

Rating _____

Reason(s) _____

_____

self-assessment scales for working in groups and working individually.

Another key to effective group work is to make sure students are clear about the purpose of working in groups. Specifically, it is important to write down objectives for the work—the topic or focus of each group's work, any pertinent instructions, and what each group should have accomplished as a result of working together.

Group work is also a time to nurture students' leadership skills. A straightforward way to do this is to ask each group to identify someone who will be the leader for the group's activities for the day. The leader's role can be viewed in many ways, and perhaps that's the point of having different students serve in this role on a rotating basis throughout the semester or year. Students and teachers alike will find that students bring their differing strengths, perspectives, and personalities to the role of group leader. This approach can be as valuable to those students who are *not* serving as group leaders as it is to those who are. By observing how different students handle this responsibility, students will see that there is more than one way to be an effective leader and perhaps be inspired to take on a leadership role themselves.

Seat Work and Teacher-Led Activities

Small-group work is becoming more and more commonplace in U.S. schools, but whole-class instruction is still a valid and necessary approach. Similarly, students need opportunities to work alone, whether writing, reading, completing assignments, taking tests, or simply thinking about how to approach a specific task. The common denominator of seat work and teacher-led activities is that, generally speaking, students remain in their seats.

Recommendations for Classroom Practice

We recommend that teachers in both elementary and secondary classrooms use the following strategies:

- Setting expectations for students working in their seats
- Maintaining students' attention during teacher-led activities

Setting Expectations for Students Working in Their Seats

One obvious expectation while students are working in their seats is that noise be minimized. This is particularly important as students finish their work, when it's easy for noise and talking to become disruptive for others still working. A common approach is to create a list of fun but worthwhile activities for students to select from when they have completed their

primary work. You might also offer some kind of reward for additional work that students complete beyond what is required. Figures 6.1 and 6.2 provide examples of lists you might post in your classroom.

Another option is to nurture students' love of learning so that class work is viewed not as unpleasant but as something to look forward to. One way to do this is to set up a creative, fun, and engaging classroom library where students can go whenever they have completed the primary task of the day. The library can include any number of focus areas, such as opportunities to read, writing stations, research and investigation opportunities to study a topic in depth, or an "Everyone Is an Expert" center where students can study something they find especially interesting.

Maintaining Students' Attention During Teacher-Led Activities

There are a number of strategies you can use to maintain students' attention during teacher-led activities and presentations.

Quick Polls. When posing general questions to the whole class, ask students to use "thumbs up or thumbs down" to indicate whether they understand the question. Follow up with additional questions if students indicate "thumbs down" or if they don't put their thumbs up or down.

Figure 6.1

Additional Work, Games, and Activities for Students

Things to Do When You Have Completed Your Task or Work

Read
- Three poems
- A chapter in a book
- A story in a magazine
- An encyclopedia page

Design
- A word-hunt puzzle
- A mobile about a story
- The perfect reading place
- An award for a classmate

Draw
- A picture of yourself
- A scene from a dream
- A machine of the future
- Definitions of four words

Write
- A letter to someone
- A poem about a friend
- Five math word problems
- A story about your school

Make
- A map of your school
- A bookmark for a friend
- A book jacket for a book
- A diagram of your classroom

List
- Outdoor sounds you hear
- Classroom sounds you hear
- Smells on your way to school
- Things you'd like to do today

Figure 6.2

Free-Time Projects

- Choose an activity from the top-priority folders (*include handouts, instructions for content-area work related to standards that are the focus of the month or semester*).
- Go to the Writer's Workshop Center.
- Write a letter.
- Do a math challenge problem.
- Study spelling.
- Work on the computer.
- Visit the math center.
- Write in a journal.

Countdowns and Call-Outs. Give a "5, 4, 3, 2, 1" cue for quiet and group attention, reinforced with comments such as "Please turn your voice off for now, Tina" or "I will wait until the class is ready to begin" and then list the names of those who are ready to continue as students are quiet and focused. For example, you might say, "I see that Jason, Deanne, Amber, and Rosie are ready . . . and Brad and Jade . . . thank you . . . OK, and Annie and Nicholas."

Random Drawings. Select readers and information-presenters during group discussions with a variation on drawing straws. Using colored magic markers, color code one end of a set of Popsicle sticks—one color for readers, another color for information presenters. As you or a selected student holds the sticks so the colored end can't be seen, the other students pick one each. The advantage of this approach is that the randomness of the selection process keeps students involved in both the discussion and their role as presenters.

Student Assistants. Ask students to come up and point to correct answers on an overhead image. The advantage of this approach is that students typically are eager to do this, and it allows you to conduct a discussion from some place other than the front of the room.

■ Section Reflection

Checking Your Understanding

Use the space provided to write your answers to the questions.

• You feel lucky this year. You don't have as many students in your class as last year, and from what you know about them, this class of students is going to be easy. Should you approach rules and procedures differently with this class? If so, why and how? If not, why not?

• You have established a set of rules and procedures for your class. But now you need to find ways to reinforce these expectations and develop student buy-in. What are some of the things you might do?

- When students arrive at class each day, they spend too much time whispering and goofing off. What is one strategy you might use to get them on task immediately?

- Whenever students line up to leave the classroom, you find that you have to spend too much time getting everyone focused, in line, and ready to go. What are some strategies you might use to practice this routine and to ease the transition?

- You are a 4th grade teacher. One of your closest friends, a first-year high school teacher, wants your advice about setting rules and procedures. What should you tell him? And how might the expectations you set for your students differ from those he might set for his students?

A Self-Assessment

Circle the number on the scale that best matches your situation, with 0 indicating "Not at all" and 4 indicating "To a great extent."

I set rules and procedures that are clear, specific, and succinct.

Not at all   To a great extent
0   1   2   3   4

I ensure that students are aware of and clear about the rules and procedures for our classroom.

Not at all   To a great extent
0   1   2   3   4

I ensure that students understand the reasons and rationale behind the rules and procedures established for our classroom.

Not at all   To a great extent
0   1   2   3   4

The rules and procedures I have established contribute to a better managed and more effective learning environment in the classroom.

Not at all   To a great extent
0   1   2   3   4

The strategies I use to reinforce rules and procedures are effective.

Not at all   To a great extent
0   1   2   3   4

2

DISCIPLINE AND CONSEQUENCES

In well-managed classrooms, teachers simultaneously develop a set of rules and procedures and a companion set of consequences and rewards related to discipline. Both sets are contained within, and driven by, the building-level management system, which allows teachers to individualize rules, procedures, consequences, and rewards for the special needs of their own classrooms. Applied properly, the interplay between rules and procedures on the one hand and discipline, consequences, and rewards on the other can foster the development of positive relationships between students and teachers and create a productive learning environment in the classroom.

Although the term discipline brings to mind strategies for punishing students, in fact, Marzano (2003) makes a strong case that disciplinary interventions should involve a balance of both positive and negative consequences. In other words, an appropriate disciplinary program involves strategies for both reinforcing positive behavior and dealing with inappropriate and disruptive behavior. The modules in this section address five key categories of disciplinary interventions that can provide a balance of positive and negative consequences:

- Module 7: Teacher Reaction
- Module 8: Tangible Rewards
- Module 9: Direct Cost
- Module 10: Group Contingency
- Module 11: Home Contingency

We should note that these classifications are somewhat artificial. Although we discuss them separately, in reality, teachers frequently use these strategies in some combination, depending on the circumstances and the students involved. Throughout these modules, therefore, you will find that some of the examples we offer are not clear-cut examples of a single approach; rather, they exemplify the point that teachers tailor and mix their strategies as needed, drawing on a variety of approaches.

■ Reflecting on Your Current Beliefs and Practices

Before reading the modules in this section, take some time to reflect on your beliefs, perspectives, and current practices regarding discipline and consequences. Then write your answers to the following questions in the space provided. Your responses will give you a basis for comparison as you read about the strategies recommended in these modules.

• Once rules and procedures have been formulated and communicated, what types of reactions, cues, and symbols do you use to acknowledge *appropriate* student behavior? What do you do to acknowledge *inappropriate* student behavior?

• What are some ways in which you "up the ante" if inappropriate, disruptive behaviors continue?

• What kinds of tangible rewards have you used? In what circumstances?

- What explicit and direct consequences do you use for inappropriate student behavior?

- What are some of the techniques you use to reward positive group behaviors and provide consequences for inappropriate group behaviors?

- Describe some ways in which you have involved parents or guardians in preventing or dealing with disciplinary situations with their children.

- Think of a time when you involved a student's parents in a behavioral issue and it resulted in improved student behavior in the classroom. Why do you think it worked?

- Think of a time when you involved a student's parents and it did not result in improved student behavior in the classroom. Why do you think it didn't work?

Teacher Reaction

Teacher reaction includes the verbal and physical reactions that indicate to students that a behavior is appropriate or inappropriate. These reactions consist of a variety of verbal and nonverbal cues and signals that you can use to forewarn students about inappropriate behavior or to recognize or follow up on either appropriate or inappropriate behavior. Class meetings, at which you gather students at the front of the room to set the stage for the upcoming lesson or unit, are good places to establish, practice, and rehearse cues and signals that will be used throughout the next stage of learning. If appropriate, you may also need to explain the rationale behind the specific cues and signals you will be using.

Recommendations for Classroom Practice

Here we consider two broad categories of teacher reactions:

- Reactions that address inappropriate behavior
- Reactions that reinforce appropriate behavior

Reactions That Address Inappropriate Behavior

Verbal and physical, or nonverbal, reactions are simple and straightforward ways to address unacceptable behavior. You can use verbal and nonverbal reactions alone or together, depending on the situation. In general, nonverbal cues alone are more effective at the secondary level, because secondary students have much more experience with, and are more attuned to, subtle forms of communication. For example, everyone in middle school and beyond knows what "rolling your eyes" means and that this form of communication can be effective even across a room. The following strategies include both verbal and nonverbal reactions.

Short Verbal Cues or Questions. When a student is misbehaving or appears headed for trouble, simply looking at the student and saying the student's name can make a difference. Similarly, you might simply ask, "What's going on?" For many students, this is all that's needed.

The Pregnant Pause. At both the elementary and secondary levels, one of the most effective nonverbal cues is the pregnant pause. When you observe a recurring disruptive behavior, you simply stop teaching, creating an uncomfortable silence. This strategy directs all attention in the room toward the offending student; the silence and obvious interruption to the flow of instruction can be a powerful motivator for a student to stop misbehaving. However, this strategy can backfire if the student's motivation is to compete with the teacher for the attention of the group. Therefore, when using this strategy, you should be ready to verbally confront the student in front of the audience if necessary.

Moving to the Front of the Room and Stopping Instruction. If the entire class is engaged in off-task, disruptive behavior or the level of talking and disruption is getting out of hand, you might simply move to the front of the room, stand silently, and make eye contact with individual students around the room.

Eye Contact. When a student is behaving inappropriately or breaking a class rule, simply making eye contact with the student is often enough to stop the behavior. At times, you might find that you can continue speaking with others or to the class as a whole. If this strategy is not effective, you might stop talking (use the "pregnant pause") and move closer to the student while continuing to maintain eye contact.

Subtle Gestures. Sometimes all it takes to stop inappropriate behavior is a subtle gesture such as putting your finger to your lips or slightly shaking your head. Many times, students know that they are doing something they shouldn't or that they are skirting the edges of inappropriate behavior. In these cases, you may need to do very little to signal to the student that the behavior should stop immediately.

Heading Students Off. "Heading them off" is a strategy to use with students who frequently misbehave. It involves simply taking the student aside and quietly asking, "What kind of day are you going to have today?" This question gives the student an opportunity to make a commitment to the expected behaviors or risk a time-out. Thus, the inappropriate behavior is headed off before the student ever gets a

chance to exhibit it. Management of this student from then on consists of nonverbal cues—for example, thumbs up, thumbs down, raised eyebrows, smiles, and the "OK" sign. If the student does appear headed in the wrong direction, you might simply ask, "Is this what you promised me a good day would look like?" or, when the child begins to misbehave, "How's your day going?" Getting students to reflect on their behavior by asking a simple question is a powerful management tool.

Reactions That Reinforce Appropriate Behavior

Verbal and nonverbal reactions are also effective ways to reinforce appropriate and productive student behavior. As with reactions to inappropriate behavior, you can use these alone or together, depending on the situation.

Short Verbal Affirmations. Acknowledging and reinforcing positive student behavior doesn't require a long speech or conversation; in fact, here we might say that "a little goes a long way." For example, you might simply say, "Thank you," "That's great," "Good job," or "Very good" when a student is engaged in positive behavior or following through on a promised action.

Smiles, Winks, and Other Signals. Nonverbal cues can effectively signal positive feedback. A smile, a thumbs-up sign, a wink, or the thumb-and-forefinger "A-OK" loop all signify approval of student behavior. Students look forward to these signs of approval. Positive nonverbal cues are important at all grade levels because they powerfully reinforce the balance of dominance and collaboration that teachers need to establish and maintain in an effectively managed classroom. Middle and high school students, some of whom are uncomfortable with verbal praise, especially appreciate these silent, anonymous cues.

Catching Students Being Good. Another intervention for acknowledging and reinforcing acceptable behavior is what Richard Curwin and Allen Mendler (1988) refer to in their book *Discipline with Dignity* as "catching students being good" (p. 97). You can use this strategy seamlessly during instruction, seat work, lab work, or group work. It is a semi-private "quick hit" strategy that involves subtly recognizing and acknowledging positive student behavior through a note, a brief aside, or a nonverbal cue as the lesson ebbs and flows. A prime opportunity to use this strategy is whenever you are circulating around the classroom. This strategy is situational, so it is important to take advantage of instances that provide a moment of semi-privacy with an individual student or a group of students. "Catching students being good" is a powerful construct for positive teacher-student relationships and flows from a teacher's sense of "withitness" (see Section 4, "Mental Set").

Tangible Rewards

This module deals with strategies that you can use to provide students with concrete symbols or tokens for appropriate behavior. As with teacher reactions, you can also withhold these tokens in response to inappropriate behavior. It is important to explain the meaning of the tokens along with the rationale behind using them. Another critical point about tangible rewards is to continually monitor your use of them to ensure that students do not view them as a bribe or a form of coercion, but rather as a healthy motivator.

Recommendations for Classroom Practice

Although teachers' use of all of the disciplinary interventions discussed in this section may vary by grade level, this variation is perhaps more true for tangible rewards. For this reason, we have divided the recommendations for this module into two sets of recommendations:

- Tangible rewards—elementary grade levels
- Tangible rewards—secondary grade levels

Tangible Rewards–Elementary Grade Levels

Teachers in elementary grades use tangible reward systems somewhat more than secondary-level teachers. These systems provide both positive and negative rewards for behavior, as the following examples show.

Points. An easy way to reward positive behavior is to give students points for behaving well. For example, one 3rd grade teacher assigns a point to each student who is on task and engaged in learning during a lesson. Each student can receive several points in a day. The top three students receive a treat at the end of the week. Each week, the process begins again.

The "Light Chart." Another approach that tangibly reinforces positive behaviors is the "light chart." If students are following the rules, their lights stay on green. Students whose behavior is disruptive or inappropriate are told to change their light to yellow (warning), red (loss of recess), or blue (loss of recess and a note home). Students who maintain a green light for the week receive a sticker. When students have accumulated a certain number of stickers—five, for example—they may choose a small toy or treat from the classroom "treasure box." An alternative is to reward students with computer coupons that they can use for free computer time—for example, to play games.

Friday Fun Club. Many elementary teachers use "Friday Fun Club" as a tangible recognition for appropriate behavior during the previous four days of class. The club meets for an hour before school lets out on Friday, and students who have earned "membership" in the club for that week play some kind of fun, educational game.

Class Posters. Class posters also can serve as concrete symbols of productive behavior. One teacher, for example, posts a large football poster that says, "Touchdown! Way to Go!" in the front of the room. The poster lists class teams and team activities that lead toward specific learning goals. Achieving a learning goal advances the team down the field. Using such posters can also reinforce a positive classroom culture. For instance, this teacher has posted a large set of hands cut from construction paper on which students can tape thank-you messages to other students. One of these, signed by "Mohammed," reads, "Erica helped me when I was hurt."

Tangible Rewards—Secondary Grade Levels

As students move from the elementary grades to middle school and then high school, the use of concrete symbols of approval and disapproval decreases markedly. Tokens and other tangible rewards are gradually replaced or used in tandem with more intrinsic, symbolic rewards. Also, secondary tangible rewards are generally delayed rather than immediate.

Verbal Praise and Critique. One middle school teacher uses verbal praise and critique almost exclusively while having students keep track of on- and off-task behavior on weekly charts that they keep at their desks and fill out daily. Each week, the teacher monitors what students write on these charts and then reviews them periodically with students. The charts are reinforced by homework-free weekends for positive behavior or a hierarchy of consequences for negative behavior. The token in this example is the behavior chart itself.

Certificates. The use of certificates to recognize both excellent behavior (such as responsibility or trustworthiness) and academic achievement (such as being named to the honor roll or the National Honor Society) is another option. The value of this kind of reward is that it can be successfully used by individual teachers, teams of teachers, specialized support teachers, elective teachers, grade-level teams, and the school or district as a whole. Using this system is also an excellent way to increase parental involvement in the school and parental awareness of what is being taught.

Reward Field Trips. Another tangible reward commonly used at the secondary level is the reward field trip. Middle school teachers and administrators often use these trips to recognize improved grade-level average GPA, students' effort and success on statewide standardized tests, and quarterly academic goals. Colorado's Cherry Creek School District, for example, holds a year-end trip for 8th grade students to a major amusement park as a reward for academic achievement and productive behavior during their final semester. Individual schools set the criteria for participation in the field trip. At one middle school, having three discipline referrals in the second semester is grounds for disqualification from this event; another school requires a minimum GPA for participation. Although criteria vary from school to school, this effort is supported by district administrators and parents alike.

Direct Cost

Direct-cost strategies involve negative consequences for student behavior rather than positive consequences. More specifically, they involve an explicit and direct consequence for inappropriate behavior; generally, they are immediately applied once a behavior has progressed beyond a point where nonverbal and verbal interventions can be effective. Direct-cost strategies usually consist of mild punishments and are used at all grade levels. However, the hierarchy of direct-cost measures can range from a brief time-out to expulsion from school, and these measures are generally applied and validated by classroom, building, and district rules and policies. Direct-cost strategies should be age appropriate, properly applied, clearly communicated, and consistent with required behaviors.

Recommendations for Classroom Practice

Teachers' use of direct-cost strategies varies somewhat from the early grades to the later grades. For these reasons, we've divided the recommendations in this module into two subsections:

- Direct cost—elementary level
- Direct cost—secondary level

Direct Cost–Elementary Level

Elementary-level teachers typically can use direct-cost strategies more effectively in the classroom than can secondary teachers. Here we review two main strategies for the elementary level—isolation time-out and overcorrection—although these can be adapted for use at the secondary level as well.

Isolation Time-Out. Sometimes the appropriate response to a student's inappropriate behavior is to remove the student from the situation or from the classroom. One common approach, particularly at the elementary level, is to create a "time-out seat" in the classroom. One teacher, for example, has set aside a seat in the corner of the room for this purpose. The teacher has posted a set of rules and consequences that students have developed with her, and the consequences for "disturbing others" are listed on a poster as follows:

1. Warning
2. Time-out seat
3. Go to office

A school or grade-level team might also set aside an area outside of the classroom for time-out situations. For example, a school might designate a small office just outside of the principal's or assistant principal's office as a time-out room, or a seat near the school secretary's desk as a time-out seat.

Overcorrection. Another useful strategy is overcorrection. This approach involves engaging the student in an activity that overcompensates for the misbehavior. In other words, the student must help return the object or environment to a condition that is better than it was before. One advantage of this approach is that it helps the student to practice a positive behavior. The following examples show how overcorrection strategies might be used:

• A student who has ripped the pages of a book is required to repair all of the torn or damaged books in the classroom.

• A student who has drawn on the classroom wall is required to erase and clean marks on *all* of the walls of the classroom.

• A student who has thrown food in the cafeteria must not only clean up the resulting mess but also help clean up spilled drinks and food in a larger area.

• A student who has damaged a piece of classroom equipment must prepare and deliver a talk to the entire class about the importance of respecting others' property, the costs involved in repairing damaged classroom equipment, and ways to protect the longevity and usefulness of the equipment.

Direct Cost—Secondary Level

As students move from elementary school to middle and high school, the most effective direct-cost strategies become those that take advantage of students' developmental needs. During adolescence and early adulthood, students begin to depend less on adults as both authority figures and role models, and more on peers and friends as primary emotional supporters and "significant others." In short, students in secondary classes are becoming independent from, and sometimes resentful of, adult influence. This shift can lead to a significant increase in defiant, insubordinate, and challenging behaviors that younger students generally do not display. Thus, direct-cost strategies that remove students from their peers, and audience, are used most often.

For example, chronically tardy students might be assigned to Saturday School, a teacher-supervised study hall. Students who are consistently tardy or off task or who refuse to complete class work must come to school for four hours on one Saturday a month. Teacher tutoring is provided, and students may be assigned this consequence for multiple Saturdays. Work completed during Saturday School is graded and included in overall student grades. Parents sign a permission form for students to participate, and they provide transportation when necessary.

Most secondary-level direct-cost techniques tend to be formalized; for example, they are published in parent/student handbooks, driven by district and building policies, and applied to everyone. Another characteristic of these strategies at the secondary level is that they tend to be natural consequences: forgetting to do homework results in no credit, failing an exam means a lower grade, getting poor grades means not going to a college of choice, and so on. At both middle and high school levels, direct-cost strategies are designed to negatively reinforce students who fail to self-regulate their own behavior at the expense of others. Time-out, exclusion from class, and expulsion from school all have the effect of removing disruptive students from their peers.

Group Contingency

This module deals with techniques that you can apply to more than one student. In *Classroom Management That Works*, Marzano (2003) describes two broad categories of group contingency strategies. *Interdependent* group contingency strategies are those in which the entire group gets a reward only when every student in the group meets the expectation for behavior. *Dependent* group contingency strategies are those in which the group's reward depends on the actions of one student or a small group of students. For obvious reasons, we favor the use of interdependent group contingency strategies. Although peer pressure can be used productively in dependent group contingency situations, students can become upset and embarrassed about being singled out. At a minimum, dependent group contingency strategies should be used only after careful reflection. For these reasons, this module describes only interdependent group contingency approaches.

Recommendations for Classroom Practice

Specific ways to use interdependent group contingency techniques vary from the early grades to the later grades, so we have divided the recommendations in this module into two subsections: interdependent group contingency techniques—elementary level and inter-dependent group contingency techniques—secondary level.

Interdependent Group Contingency Techniques—Elementary Level

Interdependent group contingency techniques apply to pre-established sets of academic and behavioral expectations that students working in pairs or larger groups are expected to follow. It is the uniqueness of a group situation that makes these techniques valuable. In most group situations, the teacher determines group membership, assigns group roles to individuals, describes a task and outcomes, and sets behavior expectations. By creating this interdependency, the teacher can monitor and facilitate group actions and interactions as if the group were a single entity. As a result, a system of rewards and consequences for group productivity and behavior becomes an effective management tool.

The ways to use interdependent group contingency strategies vary. One straightforward strategy involves placing a mark or tally on the board by a group or team name when the group is behaving as desired. Fostering an atmosphere of healthy competition and positive peer pressure can be a productive way to motivate students and manage the classroom.

One kindergarten teacher has students work in pairs with colored Uniflex blocks to design and describe patterns. Students discuss and agree on a pattern to show to the class. They write a description of the pattern on a poster using alphabet letters (for example, ABABAB, AAABBB, ABCABCABC) and then assemble the colored blocks accordingly. They then present both the written and visual patterns to the class. The group roles assigned include Poster Presenter and Pattern Presenter. Behavioral expectations are cooperation, teamwork, and sharing the blocks. The group reward for successful presentations is a tangible reward (such as a choice of their favorite sticker from a set of stickers or a "free pass" to use a segment of the class time to color or draw on their own).

A 3rd grade teacher rewards groups who are on task and behaving appropriately with a marble from the marble jar every day. When a group has collected five marbles, each student in the group is entitled to lunch with the teacher. The teacher also uses this "marbles in a jar" technique with the whole class. She puts a marble in a jar when she observes appropriate behavior and takes a marble out of the same jar when she observes inappropriate behavior. The teacher can monitor the overall learning atmosphere of the classroom simply by looking at the relative number of marbles in the jar. Using tokens in this way helps prevent any idea that they are bribes or symbols of coercion.

A 5th grade social studies teacher has groups work to create a Wild West Rendezvous activity (such as panning for gold, making candles, setting up a trading post). Groups then share the activities with students from another 5th grade class who pay with fake currency to participate in the activities. Groups use the currency to buy prizes and treats after the

Rendezvous. Groups who work together to create attractive and engaging Rendezvous activities generally make the most "money." Thus, a built-in group contingency reward and consequence system is woven throughout the whole experience.

Interdependent Group Contingency Techniques—Secondary Level

Like group contingency techniques at the elementary level, these techniques can be effective with older students. Other dynamics may need to be given more consideration, however.

For example, one middle school science teacher has students work in groups to practice the scientific method. Students observe a phenomenon (such as soap dispersing in water, convection, or a chemical reaction). They then develop a hypothesis, set up an experiment, collect and display data, draw conclusions, publish their findings, and present the experiment to their classmates. The group contingency technique that the teacher uses is to grade the entire group on both the academic task and their effective group interactions. All members of the group receive the same individual grade as the group grade. Thus the teacher uses peer pressure to reinforce appropriate group behaviors. This teacher also recognizes that some students do not or cannot work effectively in groups and allows any member of the class to choose to do the assignment alone. The expectations for groups and solo students are identical with respect to outcomes, and the workload is the same for both. Therefore, the teacher takes advantage of the mutual self-interest that a division of labor can provide for those who choose to work in a group.

For secondary school teachers, we recommend caution in using interdependent group contingency techniques that require a whole class to meet a behavioral criterion and that have a negative group consequence if one member of the class fails to perform. Older students have a well-developed sense of fairness and may strongly object to receiving a consequence for someone else's behavior. By holding an entire class responsible and accountable for the actions of a few, you may compromise students' trust in justice at the expense of equity.

Home Contingency

Making parents aware of both positive and negative behaviors of their children can be a powerful management tool. Home contingency techniques take advantage of two synergistic factors. First, parents have a strong and continuous interest in the physical, emotional, and academic well-being of their children. Simply stated, parents want their children to do well in school. No parent sends a child out the door to school, or anywhere else, hoping that the child will have a bad experience there. Second, parents are the most significant adult in a child's life and maintain that status whether the family is intact or not. In a child's mind, the desire for parental approval far exceeds the desire for teacher approval. Therefore, teachers, as effective classroom managers, must take advantage of every opportunity to build a solid partnership with parents, the most behaviorally influential people in students' lives.

Recommendations for Classroom Practice

Our recommendations for this module fall into two categories:

* Making parents aware of their children's behavior
* Establishing a system of consequences to be administered at home

Making Parents Aware of Their Children's Behavior

As many of the following examples illustrate, a critical aspect of interacting with parents about their children's behavior is developing a relationship with parents even before school begins. As we describe in Section 6, "Getting Off to a Good Start," contacting parents early in the year, or perhaps before the school year begins, lays a good foundation for positive relationships with parents.

Phone Calls. When a behavior issue arises and parental contact is appropriate, calling the parent is one of the easiest and most straightforward actions you can take. One 2nd grade teacher calls each parent at the beginning of the school year. She introduces herself and tells the parent that she is delighted to have the child in her class and that she will be calling periodically to inform the parent about the child's progress. She asks the parent if the child has any special needs or concerns about school and briefly explains the format for upcoming parent conferences. This helps establish a positive parent-teacher relationship; in the event of a phone call about negative behavior, the teacher already has a relationship with the parent.

For example, when a student is continually misbehaving in the classroom and the teacher's efforts to correct the behavior have not worked, she might call the parent. By talking the problem over with the parent, she might learn of something that is troubling the student at home or get an idea for a strategy that might work with the student. In addition, the parent can talk with the child about the issue at home, find out if something is bothering the student, and reinforce the need for productive classroom behavior.

Conference Calls with Parents. A 9th grade English teacher holds monthly conference calls with parents of students who are performing below expectations (behavioral or academic). Students are present for these conferences and have an opportunity to explain why their performance is below standards set by the teacher. Specific action plans and consequences are discussed and modified as necessary, and follow-up dates are confirmed. Students who fail to participate in these conferences are referred to the office for administrative consequences associated with insubordination. These can range from detention to suspension from school.

Parent-Teacher-Student Conferences. A kindergarten teacher holds regular conferences with parents throughout the year. When she has a particular issue to discuss, she asks that the student attend. An important element of her approach is that she holds a conference with the parents of each student *before* the child starts school. The parents bring the child to the conference, and the child and the teacher meet one-on-one for a while. The teacher orients the child to the room, the school, the nurse's office, and the cafeteria and introduces the child to the principal. During this orientation, the teacher also goes over

behavior expectations with the child and the child's parents.

Orientation Packets. One 5th grade teacher sends an orientation packet home with students on the first day of school. The packet includes a set of behavior expectations that she and her teammates have agreed upon. These expectations apply to all students in all 5th grade classes, and related behaviors are monitored and recorded weekly by students. The students take copies of the behavior record home in their Friday Folder, which includes notes to the parents as well.

Similarly, a middle school science teacher sends a set of expectations for classroom and laboratory behavior home with students on the first day of school. The teacher asks parents to review the expectations with the student, sign the form, and return it to the teacher. On the second day of school, students take a brief quiz on both the classroom expectations and the safety requirements for laboratory work. The teacher makes a phone call to parents who either didn't sign the form or whose student didn't return the form.

Parent Orientation Activities. A middle school English-as-a-Second-Language teacher sends an invitation to parents to attend a breakfast orientation at school. Translators are available, and the teacher goes over the student handbook in detail. She emphasizes the culture of U.S. schools and has copies of the handbook available in several languages. She follows up this orientation with bimonthly breakfast meetings to keep parents connected to the school and to provide a forum for them to exchange views and concerns. She uses these days as an opportunity to have informal conferences with parents about student behavior.

Notes to Parents. A 1st grade student repeatedly had been off task, talking, interrupting, tattling, walking around the room, and covering her ears during directions (pouting and being noncommunicative). The teacher sent home daily progress notes regarding behavior, and the child was isolated to a desk in the classroom whenever these behaviors occurred. The teacher held a sit-down conference with the parents and the child every two weeks, and the teacher reviewed behavior and improvements during the interval.

Establishing a System of Consequences to Be Administered at Home

Establishing partnerships with parents can be a highly effective way to reinforce positive student behavior and correct negative or unacceptable behavior, particularly when other approaches haven't worked. Developing a good strategy usually begins with a face-to-face meeting with the student's parents. During the meeting, you should explain what has been going on and the strategies you have tried in the classroom. Together, you and the student's parents can talk about and identify consequences to be enacted at home for both positive and negative behavior. For example, one 10th grade teacher solicits parents' support by asking them to make the son's or daughter's driving privileges contingent on classroom behavior. The teacher uses this approach only for students who are chronically disruptive or unproductive in their work. Parents get a weekly telephone report on behavior and effort in class.

Some situations will involve parents but will require especially creative solutions. Here, the teacher—and perhaps school administrators—will need to draw on their combined knowledge, experience, and skills to craft appropriate responses. For example, at one middle school, two students were "cussing out" the Middle Eastern teaching assistant in Spanish and making fun of her as she supervised lunch recess. A Spanish interpreter was brought in and asked to inform the girls about the impropriety of addressing adults in that fashion. The interpreter stressed cultural togetherness of the students and school staff and conveyed this message to the Spanish-speaking parents as well. The girls apologized to the adult, and their parents put disciplinary consequences into effect at home.

■ Section Reflection

Checking Your Understanding

Use the space provided to write your answers to the questions.

- Several students in your class are very quiet individuals who don't speak much in class. Your experience and intuition tell you that you need to be especially sensitive to keeping your interactions with them private. What disciplinary approaches might you tend to use with these students? And how might you best acknowledge positive and productive behavior?

- A student in your class admits that he was mad one day and ruined several books with a black permanent marker. How might you deal with this situation?

- The students in your class don't seem to think much of tangible rewards like stickers, candy, and gum. What are some other concrete symbols you might use to acknowledge productive behavior?

• We discussed the advantages of using interdependent group contingency strategies. What might be one disadvantage or caution about using this approach?

• Over the past couple of weeks, you have had to send Gabriella to the classroom time-out seat three times because of her disruptive behavior. But the behavior has continued. What are some ways in which you might deal with this situation? Under what circumstances would you contact Gabriella's parents?

• One of your 2nd grade students threw a rock at and struck a substitute P.E. teacher in response to a dare from another student. How might you deal with this situation?

A Self-Assessment

Circle the number on the scale that best matches your situation, with 0 indicating "Not at all" and 4 indicating "To a great extent."

I have a set of verbal and nonverbal cues and signals that I use to forewarn students about inappropriate behavior and to recognize or follow up on either appropriate or inappropriate behavior.

Not at all   To a great extent

   0   1   2   3   4

Whenever I use tangible rewards, I take care to ensure that students understand the rationale behind their use and that I consistently apply these rewards.

Not at all   To a great extent

   0   1   2   3   4

The group contingency strategies I use result in more effective, productive group work.

Not at all   To a great extent

   0   1   2   3   4

I communicate with parents regarding positive *and* negative aspects of their children's behavior and participation in class.

Not at all   To a great extent

   0   1   2   3   4

I have clearly shared the various disciplinary approaches, and the rationale behind them, with students as well as parents.

Not at all   To a great extent

   0   1   2   3   4

3

TEACHER-STUDENT RELATIONSHIPS

Many people believe that the relationship between teacher and student is the starting place for good classroom management. This makes good intuitive sense. If the teacher has a good relationship with students, all of the other aspects of classroom management will run much more smoothly.

One of the more promising aspects of the teacher-student relationship is that it is not a function of what teachers *feel*. Rather, it is a function of what teachers *do*. More specifically, students cannot see inside a teacher's head to determine the teacher's thoughts. They can't see if a teacher is having positive or negative thoughts about the class as a whole or an individual student. Rather, students look at the teacher's behaviors and interpret those behaviors as signs of the teacher's attitude about the class or an individual student. As researcher Theo Wubbels and his colleagues (Wubbels, Brekelmans, van Tartwijk, & Admiral, 1999) note

> We consider every behavior that someone displays in the presence of someone else as a communication, and therefore we assume that in the presence of someone else one cannot *not* communicate. . . . Whatever someone's intentions are, the other persons in the communication will infer meaning from that someone's behavior. If, for example, teachers ignore students' questions, perhaps because they do not hear them, then students may not only get this inattention but also infer that the teacher is too busy or thinks that the students are too dull to understand or that the questions are impertinent. The message that the students take from the teacher's negation can be different from the teacher's intention. (pp. 153–154, emphasis in original)

We say this is a positive circumstance because it implies that the classroom teacher can forge a positive relationship with every student regardless of how the teacher feels about the students in the class. In other words, a teacher does not have to personally feel connected to create the perception of connectedness to every student. The teacher does not have to feel interested in every student to create the perception of interest in every student.

The modules in this section are about the specific things you can do to create optimal teacher-student relationships—optimal in the sense that the relationships provide a foundation on which you can best carry out the challenging task of teaching and students can best carry out the challenging task of learning. This section has four modules:

- Module 12: Demonstrating Personal Interest in Students
- Module 13: Behaving Equitably and Responding Affirmatively to Questions
- Module 14: Exhibiting an Assertive Connection
- Module 15: Being Aware of the Needs of Different Types of Students

■ Reflecting on Your Current Beliefs and Practices

Before reading the modules in this section, take some time to reflect on your beliefs and perspectives about teacher-student relationships and any actions you take in this area. Then write your answers to the following questions in the space provided. Your responses will give you a basis for comparison as you read about the strategies recommended in these modules.

- In terms of classroom management, why is it important to develop effective relationships with students?

- What things do you do to develop good relationships with your students?

• What do you do to learn about individual students' interests?

• Are your interactions with all students equitable? What specific things do you do to ensure that they are?

• How would you characterize your communication style with students?

• How effective do you think you are in communicating with students?

• How aware are you of the needs of different students in your classes?

• What kinds of information do you routinely collect to learn more about high-needs students in your classes?

Demonstrating Personal Interest in Students

Like everyone, students want to feel that they are "known"—that others understand them, appreciate them, and recognize their unique qualities, skills, interests, needs, and personalities. Teachers who understand this and consciously find ways to demonstrate that they are interested in students will build a stronger foundation for effective classroom management and learning.

Recommendations for Classroom Practice

There are numerous ways to show interest in students as individuals. In this module, we discuss three broad strategies:

- Discovering and incorporating students' personal interests into academics
- Noticing individual accomplishments and important events in students' lives
- Interacting with students as individuals

Discovering and Incorporating Students' Personal Interests into Academics

As effective and experienced teachers know, for many students, success in school and the degree of their engagement in learning are highly dependent on how relevant, meaningful, and interesting they find the content they are learning. Even at an intuitive level, this makes sense, particularly when it comes to abstract concepts that initially seem to have little to do with day-to-day life.

There are many ways to learn about students' personal interests, including the following:

- Student interest surveys
- Teacher-student conferences
- Informal conversations with students
- Taking notice of the kinds of activities students participate in outside of school

Figure 12.1 is an example of a survey you can use at the beginning of the year to learn about students' interests.

Teacher-student conferences also offer great opportunities for learning about students' interests. Some students are quite verbal and outspoken about their likes, dislikes, and interests; others are not. But you can gently tease out these personal interests as you build relationships with students throughout the year. Asking students questions is one obvious way to learn about their interests, but some students (just like adults) may not realize the full range of their interests. To learn

Figure 12.1

Student Interest Survey

As we begin the school year, it's important for me to learn a little bit about you. Each one of us is unique! Thank you for helping me learn more about you.

1. Do you have any hobbies? If so, what are they? (For example, collecting baseball cards or stuffed animals? Drawing or painting? Building things?) _____
_____

2. Do you participate in sports? If so, which sport (or sports)? _____
What do you like best about doing this? _____

3. Do you take lessons of any kind? If so, what kind? (For example, music, art, singing, speech) _____
_____

4. One person you especially admire is _____ because _____
_____

5. What kinds of things did you do over the summer or on vacation that you enjoyed? _____
_____

6. What is your favorite book, game, movie, or television show? _____

7. If you had to describe yourself in a sentence or two, what might you say that would help a person learn something about your personal interests? _____
_____
_____

8. Complete each of these sentences:

a. During my free time, I like to _____
b. One thing I really like to do with friends is _____
c. I really enjoy _____
d. Our family enjoys _____
e. If I had a month of Saturdays, I'd spent most of my time _____
f. Some day I'd like to be _____
g. The subject I like most in school is _____
h. I like this subject best because _____

about—and spark—students' interests, consider using these strategies:

- Ask which book, article, video, or movie the student most enjoyed in the past month.
- Give the student a leadership role in the classroom.
- Ask the student to suggest a video or movie clip for the class to watch that exemplifies a particular topic or idea.
- Assign the student the task of caring for a class or school pet (such as a turtle or fish).
- Ask students to line up for lunch or to sit in groups in fun ways; for example, ask them whether they would rather "travel to the moon in a rocket ship," "go for a long drive in the countryside," "lie in a hammock and read a good book," or "sail across the ocean."
- Give students options for topics to study; for example, during a unit on historical investigation, the options might include "scientific discoveries of the past," "young people who were inventors or entrepreneurs," "the discovery of new animals or plants," and "how rain forest plants, fungi, and herbs have been successfully used for medicinal or healing purposes."

You can incorporate students' interests into academics in many ways. When you design lessons and units around writing and reading standards, for example, you can allow students to choose topics that interest them. For example, during a unit about classical music, have students evaluate their own favorite music against the criteria for classical music (such as test of time; the artist is a master of the medium).

Then ask them to share their music and evaluations with each other.

Noticing Individual Accomplishments and Important Events in Students' Lives

Another highly useful way to ensure that students feel known and appreciated is to notice their participation in sports, drama, and other extracurricular activities—as well as important family events—and to appropriately comment on these activities. You can develop a number of practices in this area:

- Use part of each parent-teacher conference to ask about and listen for critical details, such as upcoming family get-togethers or vacations, transition points for siblings (such as graduation, marriage), or a move to a new home.
- Develop good relationships with teachers of "specials" and learn about the extracurricular activities students are participating in throughout the school year.
- Read the school newspaper, newsletter, and bulletins for information and announcements about students who are participating in extracurricular activities. These are excellent sources of information about a variety of activities, including track or swim meets; debates; basketball, softball, and football games; clubs; school performances; and community volunteer activities.
- Compliment students on important achievements in and outside of school. This may include commenting (and offering congratulations, when appropriate) on an achievement in another class, such as a well-written

paper, an engaging class presentation, or a class-helper role that a student has assumed. It may also include offering positive feedback when students are involved in community projects, such as a local recycling effort, a book drive at their church or synagogue, or volunteering at an animal shelter or a soup kitchen.

Interacting with Students as Individuals

It almost goes without saying that interacting with students as individuals is important if you want to demonstrate that you are personally interested in them. Here are a few straightforward things that you can do and practice so that students feel you know them as individuals:

• Meet students at the door as they come into class and say hello to each student, *being sure to use the student's first name.* Simply saying "hello" or "good morning" to groups of students does not have the same impact as saying, "Good morning, Rosa," "Hi, Joseph," "Welcome, Susan," and so on.

• Find time to talk informally with students about their lives and their interests. These kinds of opportunities occur naturally over the course of a day or a week—for example, with students who arrive early to class or as students complete a classroom task at different times. This is a good time to give students unsolicited "strokes" regarding work, dress, hair, athletic accomplishments, or personal interests. You also might ask their opinions about the unit you are teaching, ask about their successes in other classes, or pass on compliments that you have heard about them from other teachers. If and when appropriate, give the student a hug.

• Make a positive phone call home with the student present.

• Take photos of students for room display.

• Attend an after-school function that involves the student.

• Single out a couple of students each day—for example, in the lunchroom—and talk with them. This can be as simple as beginning a conversation by saying, "How's your day going, John?" "What did you think about the class discussion today, Amber?" "Hi, Liana. Looks like it's going to be a sunny weekend. Do you have any plans?" "Hi, Jose. Are you excited about the play this weekend?" "Thanks for offering that explanation today in class, Mariana. I think it helped make things clearer for everyone."

• Greet students *by name* outside of school if you happen to run into them at, say, the movie theater, a sporting event, or the grocery store. A long discussion is not necessary; just a give a warm greeting that uses the student's name: "Hi, Alex. Nice to see you," "Hi, Meg. Enjoy the game!" or "Have a good weekend, Ben."

Behaving Equitably and Responding Affirmatively to Questions

Another key to fostering effective relationships with students is ensuring that classroom interactions are equitable and positive. Students who see that teachers are interacting with them in affirming, positive ways—and that they are interacting with all students equitably—are more likely to approach learning with a positive attitude.

As described in *Classroom Management That Works* (Marzano, 2003), one of the most popular professional development programs is Teacher Expectations and Student Achievement, or TESA. Extensive descriptions of this program and its components are available elsewhere (see, for example, http://streamer.lacoe. edu/tesa/). Briefly, this research-based program is based on teacher expectation theory. According to Good (1987), teacher expectations are "inferences that teachers make about the future behavior or academic achievement of their students based on what they know about these students now" (p. 32). Students are more likely to feel accepted and valued when teachers use behaviors that are equitable toward all students.

Another source of strategies for enhancing teacher-student relationships is the work of Madeline Hunter (1969). Among the many topics she addressed, questioning was particularly pertinent to the teacher-student relationship. When a teacher asks a question about academic content and a student responds incorrectly, how the teacher interacts with the student conveys a powerful negative or positive message. Some actions might communicate to students that it is better for them not to respond if they aren't sure their answer is correct. Other actions tend to communicate to students that any response they have is welcome, but they are responsible for providing thoughtful responses.

Recommendations for Classroom Practice

Building on some aspects of TESA and of Hunter's work, as well as our own experiences in classrooms across the country, in this module we highlight three broad categories of strategies you can use to convey that you are approaching students equitably:

- Physical gestures and movements
- Positive interaction strategies
- Affirmative reactions to incorrect responses

Physical Gestures and Movements

Even without speaking you can do a few straightforward things to convey that all students are equal and all students are important. As we describe in Section 4, "Mental Set," many of these same behaviors communicate to students that you are aware of everything that is going on in the classroom.

Eye Contact. We all like to feel that our presence is noted. Stated negatively, if we feel that someone doesn't even acknowledge our presence we tend to interpret this as a sign of disrespect. Students react the same way. They want and need some sign that the teacher acknowledges their presence in class. One simple way to do this is to ensure that you make eye contact with every student. Scan the entire room as you speak, looking into every student's eyes as you do so. Avoid making darting glances around the room or looking over the heads of students. If possible, try to make sure that every student has made eye contact with you as well. However, in doing so you must be sensitive to cultural differences. In some cultures, it is a sign of disrespect for students to make eye contact with the teacher.

Moving Around the Room. An unwitting type of inequitable behavior is to stand in the front of the room. Students can interpret this as an indication that those in the front of the room are receiving more attention that those in the back. Even when you are presenting information or lecturing, you should move around the room, between rows or chairs, and ensure that you are close to individual students.

Looking and Listening. Looking at someone who is speaking and carefully listening to what that person is saying conveys that you value the speaker's words. The simple act of *actually listening* to someone can be more valuable than an extensive conversation. Even if the listener says nothing in return but nods gently in affirmation, or simply responds, "Thank you," the speaker can feel acknowledged and heard.

Positive Interaction Strategies

In addition to basic body movements and gestures, a number of specific strategies convey an equitable view of students:

- *Attribute ideas and comments to those who offered them.* The benefits of this practice are that it conveys respect for individual thinking and initiative and encourages students to offer ideas in the future. For example, you might say, "I'd like to thank Zach, who suggested that we talk about these two topics together since there are some common themes. Great idea, Zach." Or you might say, "Thank you for your comments, Jen. You did a great job of summarizing the key points."

- *Encourage everyone's participation.* It's important to encourage every student to participate in class discussions—those who generally are eager to respond as well as those who generally are not. Students may not participate for a variety of reasons. They may feel shy speaking up in a group of students, uncertain about their responses, and fearful of negative feedback if their answer is inaccurate, or they may be disengaged or uninterested in the topic. Even with very shy students, you can find sensitive ways to engage them in the conversation. For example, as you are moving around the room during a class discussion, you might stop at a student's desk and quietly ask the student to share his thoughts or to offer an answer. A good initial way to engage a reluctant student is to ask the student to provide an answer to something that you are certain the student knows. This strategy can help build the student's confidence about speaking up in class in the future.

- *Provide appropriate "wait time."* A strategy that relates to the simple act of listening is to provide appropriate "wait time" for students to respond to questions or prompts. Some students are immediately ready to participate; others need time to think and reflect. At times it can be useful to provide additional wait time even if one or two frequent participants raise their hands immediately. To encourage other students to participate, you might simply say, "OK. Thank you, Ian and Elena. I'm going to give everyone a couple of minutes to think about this, and then I'll ask for responses again."

Affirmative Reactions to Incorrect Responses

Sometimes an affirmative reaction involves being aware of what *not* to do. To communicate to students that their responses to questions are welcome and honored, you should avoid certain behaviors when their responses are incorrect:

- *Don't tell students that they should have known the answer.* Even if you have already presented the information pertaining to a question you have asked, it is generally not a good idea to tell students that they should have known the answer to a given question. Responding in this way squelches students' desire to participate and may have the unintended consequence of embarrassing them in front of others.

- *Don't ignore a response.* When students provide responses, they should be validated for participating in the discussion. If you immediately ask another student to respond without

acknowledging the previous student's effort, you send the message that you appreciate only correct responses.

- *Avoid subjective comments about incorrect answers.* Always avoid making a subjective judgment about an incorrect answer until you fully understand the student's thinking behind the answer.

- *Don't allow negative comments from other students.* Never allow other students to comment on the quality of a student's answer unless the norm for such comments is "positive comments only!"

On the positive side, you can offer a number of responses that honor students' answers even if they are incorrect and that encourage them to respond in the future:

- *Provide correctives.* Sometimes students provide responses that are partially correct and partially incorrect. Every moment is a teaching moment; focusing attention on what's wrong wastes precious time that could be used to provide more help. Acknowledge the correct portion of the response and then explain how the incorrect portion might be altered.

- *State the question that the incorrect response answered.* For example, imagine that a teacher asks, "Who can offer an example of the use of personification?" Amy raises her hand and says, "Well, I can think of a couple—*the large, dark chair wrapped its arms around her* and *the piece of bread was hard as a rock.*" The teacher says, "Those are two great examples of figures of speech, Amy. The first one shows the use of personification; the second is an example of a simile. Good thinking."

- *Encourage collaboration.* If several students have provided incorrect responses, you might thank everyone for their answers and then say, "Thanks to everyone who offered their ideas. I can see that you are on the right track. Let's spend the next few minutes in small groups talking about this question a bit further." This approach gives students time to seek help from peers, which can result in better responses and enhance learning.

• *Restate the question.* If students are offering incorrect responses, another useful strategy is to ask the question a second time and allow time for students to think before you ask for responses again. For example, because science is so vocabulary dependent and many students don't have strong background knowledge in science terminology, it is good practice to restate questions using an analogy or a parallel question involving something that is familiar to the student. If a teacher is asking a question about the four chambers of the heart and the student is having trouble with terms such as *superior vena cava, right auricle, pulmonary arteries*, and so on, the teacher might compare the heart to a water pump. She also might diagram the parts of a water pump and then superimpose the parts of the heart over the parts of the pump.

• *Give hints and cues.* Provide enough guidance so that students gradually come up with

the answer. For example, if students are providing incorrect responses about what kind of energy is captured in a plant's leaves during photosynthesis, a teacher might say, "Think about the first part of the word *photosynthesis*. What do you need to take a photograph besides a camera?"

• *Let students opt out.* If a student is providing an answer and then becomes confused, graciously give the student an opportunity to opt out for now. For example, you might say, "OK, no problem. Do you want to think about it some more and I'll come back to you?"

• *Provide the answer and ask for elaboration.* Sometimes a student simply cannot come up with the correct answer; in this case, you might provide the answer but then ask the student to explain it in his own words or provide an example of the answer. For example, if a teacher has asked a student to define *communism*, she might give the definition in her own way, then ask the student to repeat the definition in his own terms and to compare it to his understanding of *democracy*.

• *Acknowledge the student's participation.* Above all, be sure to thank any student who takes the risk of answering a question, right or wrong, for having the initiative to do so.

Exhibiting an Assertive Connection

Over time we all develop certain tendencies in how we communicate. In the classroom, our style of communication might inadvertently work against establishing effective relationships with students. This module reviews different communication styles and, in particular, highlights the effectiveness and benefits of a communication style we call Assertive Connector.

Many authors have created categorizations of communication styles. Among them are Vicki Weatherford (1985) and Evelyn Sieburg (1972), who extensively studied communication styles, and Joyce Emde (1991), who conducted in-depth research on those styles. This module builds on the work of these authors and researchers. Specifically, in this module we address five distinct styles of communication: the Assertive Connector, the Apathetic Avoider, the Junior Therapist, the Bulldozer, and the Hider. Note that these communication styles are distinct from, though similar to, the types of behavior reviewed in Section 5, "Student Responsibility." Figure 14.1 includes brief descriptions of some of the behaviors and affects of people who exhibit these communication styles.

It can be difficult to determine why our communication works at times and doesn't work at other times. Frequently we are unaware of the subtleties of our style and how it affects

others. One reason for this lack of awareness is that our communication style involves not only our words but also our body language and gestures, our tone of voice, and the underlying message, or "meta-message," of what we are saying. A meta-message is the overall message that we are conveying or "telling" other people about how we feel about our relationship with them and what they are left with as a result of their time with us.

The first communication style, Assertive Connector, is the only one that allows for full communication, goodwill, and positive results; therefore, it is the most desirable of the communication styles we discuss. This style unites the concepts of assertiveness, personal responsibility (see Section 5, "Student Responsibility") and emotional objectivity (see Section 4, "Mental Set"). The meta-message here is "I value our relationship and what you have to say."

The second through fifth categories of communication style do not promote assertiveness, responsibility, or positive relationships and outcomes for various reasons. Although each of these four styles has aspects of nonassertiveness (for example, the Hider style and the Bulldozer style closely resemble the descriptions of "passive" and "aggressive," respectively, in the section on "Student

Figure 14.1

Five Communication Styles

The Assertive Connector

- Is not engaged in other tasks.
- Faces speaker and uses consistent eye contact.
- Mirrors the speaker's emotions; for example, if the speaker is sad, the listener's face reflects sadness.
- Spends equal time speaking and listening.
- Expresses emotions appropriately.
- Uses body language that matches the emotion being communicated.
- Asks for clarification or elaboration; asks questions respectfully.
- Deliberately attempts to fully understand the content and the emotions being expressed by the other person.
- Repeats what was said to ensure understanding (for instance, "What I heard you say is . . .").
- Can express agreement, disagreement, or neutrality.
- Engages in conversation in a win-win manner with the intention to connect with the other person and resolve any issues.
- Sends this meta-message: "I value our relationship and what you have to say."

The Apathetic Avoider

- Ignores the other person's presence or attempt to speak.
- Pauses too long before replying, barely replies, or does not reply.
- Interrupts or interjects own thoughts while the other person is speaking.
- Is distracted while working with or talking to the other person; displays distraction through body movements, such as tapping.
- Conveys being apathetic, detached, or distracted.
- Talks while the other person is talking or talks for long periods without listening.
- Does not mirror the other person; uses body language that is inconsistent with what is being said by either person.
- Turns away, looks away, or walks away.
- Avoids relationship with the other person.
- May experience considerable anxiety when attempting to connect with another person.
- Sends this meta-message: "I don't want much of a relationship with you and will put minimal effort into it."

The Junior Therapist

- Takes a one-up position—assumes that he or she is better able to speak for someone than that person is.
- Talks for the other person, telling the other how he or she feels, thinks, and acts.

(continued)

Figure 14.1

Five Communication Styles *(continued)*

- Tells the other person how he or she should feel, think, and act.
- Tends to talk about the other person rather than about himself or herself.
- Criticizes the other person for his or her feelings, thoughts, and actions.
- Decides how the other person is or should be, then responds only when the person acts in accordance with that perception.
- Tells the other person that the advice being given is for the other person's own good.
- Uses prior knowledge of the person's history in an amateur way, "analyzing" why the person feels, thinks, or acts in a particular way that benefits the speaker's point of view.
- Uses knowledge about the other person to distort that person's point of view, often to enhance his or her own argument in hopes of "winning" the conversation.
- Sends this meta-message: "I know you better than you know yourself. I know you better than I know myself."

The Bulldozer
- Focuses on own topic and ignores topics brought up by the other person.
- Switches from the other person's topic to a topic of his or her own liking; dominates the conversation.
- Repeats the same thing many times over.
- May speak in a louder-than-necessary voice, shout, or scream.
- Engages in aggressive behavior—attacks, blames, criticizes, belittles, intimidates, invalidates, or mocks the other.
- May engage in name calling, use sarcasm or use a condescending tone in an attempt to harm the other person's self-esteem or point of view and, ultimately, to "win" the conversation, making the other "lose."
- Attempts to make the other person appear incompetent, inferior, unintelligent, or childish, and implies that the other person generally lacks the positive qualities that the bulldozer believes he or she has.
- May use violence or intimidating gestures to suggest violence.
- Sends this meta-message: "I will do whatever it takes to get my way."

The Hider
- Speaks too softly for the listener to hear.
- Uses incomplete, incongruent, unclear, paradoxical, or ambiguous sentences; may talk a lot but say little.
- Uses contradictory adverbs, over-qualification, or words that indicate unclear status, such as "maybe, sort of."
- Pulls away from listener; body language conveys fearfulness or confusion.
- Doesn't respond to personal questions or says very little; "hides out" in a group.
- Body language, voice tone, and message are not congruent because the person frequently is trying to pretend that he or she is not hiding.
- Appears afraid of being heard, criticized, or confronted; assumes that he or she will "lose" the conversation and would rather leave and not continue talking.
- Sends this meta-message: "I am afraid of you and don't want you to know about me."

Responsibility"), each also has distinguishing characteristics, so the four nonassertive styles can help us better understand effective communication with students.

The place to start is to determine your dominant communication style. Pay close attention to your communications for a few days and see which style you use most often and with whom. You probably exhibit characteristics from a number of styles at different times, but you should try to identify one dominant style you think you use. Next, spend some time considering what the effects of your communication style are on you and on others. Do you like the results you are getting? Does more or less conflict result when you use one style over another?

If you are not completely satisfied with your communications, try to incorporate more aspects of the Assertive Connector style into your behavior, then re-examine the effect of your communications. See if you find your relationships have improved or if you are more comfortable. You may find that trying to change your communication style is uncomfortable for a while until you are more familiar with and adept at the Assertive Connector style. Figure 14.2 includes a chart you might use as you pay attention to and track your communications.

Figure 14.2 Tracking the Effects of My Communication Styles				
Event	Types of Behavior I Used	Meta-Message	Style	Results

Being Aware of the Needs of Different Types of Students

To understand the different types of students who enter every classroom, it is useful to consider the life circumstances of those children and adolescents who are coping with problems in varying degrees. Studies shed light on the intensity of the issues that all too many of our youth must deal with at home and at school.

Young people are affected by a wide range of mental health and behavioral issues, including eating disorders, rape, inappropriate and unhealthy sexual activity, drugs, and suicide. In addition, although we all hope—and work to ensure—that school is a safe environment in every sense, this is not always the case. For example, a report from the U.S. Department of Justice and the National Association of School Psychologists estimates that 160,000 children miss school each day because of fear of bullying (Lee, 1993). More recently, researchers have found that nearly one-third of U.S. schoolchildren are targets of bullying (Nansel et al., 2001). These and other data point to the importance of paying attention to the needs of students and doing everything possible to ensure that the school environment is safe, healthy, supportive, and productive.

Obviously, students who have experienced unhealthy life situations and mental health issues may arrive at school feeling distraught, needy, angry, hungry, fearful, confused, anxious, or apathetic, or they may display a host of other conditions that may be bewildering to the teacher. Rather then attempting to figure out the specific issues each student faces, teachers might first consider the five categories of high-needs students (see Figure 15.1), which can help teachers make distinctions regarding behavioral problems they may encounter in the classroom. Not surprisingly, given the statistics reported earlier in this module, some students may fall into diagnostic categories found in the *Diagnostic and Statistical Manual of Mental Disorders, fourth edition* (DSM IV) (American Psychiatric Association, 2000). The DSM IV is a listing of official codes for medical record-keeping, data collection, and reporting to third parties such as private insurers and the World Health Organization. Copies are available at any bookstore.

As noted, Figure 15.1 lists the five general categories of high-needs students. The sections that follow provide a description of each type and brief case study. You may notice that some of these descriptions are similar to the behavior categories described in Section 5 on "Student Responsibility." The themes of passive or

Figure 15.1
Five Categories of High-Need Students

Category	Subcategory
Passive	Fear of relationships
	Fear of failure
Aggressive	Hostile
	Oppositional
	Covert
Attention Problems	Hyperactive
	Inattentive
Perfectionist	None
Socially Inept	None

aggressive behaviors certainly are part of the descriptions of problematic students. These categories and descriptions also overlap to some extent with the communication styles described in Module 14 in this section. For further information, we recommend that you consult *Classroom Management That Works* (Marzano, 2003).

Passive Students

The category of passive is divided into two subcategories: fear of relationships and fear of failure. Students in both subcategories experience high levels of fear, but the focus of the fear is different and may have different origins. Fear of relationships may result from verbal, physical, or sexual abuse. Fear of failure may be the result of repeated failures due to undiagnosed or untreated attention deficit hyperactivity disorder (ADHD), depression, or the like. Whatever the source, the student may not be able to quickly change these feelings and the exhibited behaviors.

A student who is passive may need much more encouragement and support than other students. Comments that seem even slightly critical from the student's point of view, even comments intended to motivate the student, may negatively affect this student much more than the teacher expects. Patience and kindness go a long way.

Case Study

Allison is quite shy and assumes she cannot do regular schoolwork. She has few friends, and her grades are lower than her ability would predict. She is afraid of relationships and failure. Her teacher, Mr. Winnig, has a plan that has worked with other similar students. He does not approach Allison too quickly, but slowly and surely, through small but continual conversations, he gains her trust. When he determines that she is ready for a more in-depth conversation, he asks to speak with her after class, to avoid embarrassing her. The conversation goes something like this:

> "Allison, I want you to know that I think you are a very likeable person, and you are smart, too. I wonder if we couldn't work together to bring up your grades and maybe help you make some friends, too. What do you think?"

> Allison slowly replies that she has a hard time with everything.

"Well, I really want to help. It would just be a few conversations when no one else can hear. We can plan how to build some confidence and improve your homework. OK?"

"Yeah, I'd like that. I need a little help with stuff."

"Let's talk during recess tomorrow, OK?"

"OK."

Aggressive Students

Most teachers are familiar with the aggressive student who is a disruptive, frustrating, and clearly troubled (and troubling) person. Issues such as physical or sexual abuse; overindulgence; mood disorders such as depression, bipolar disorder, or ADHD; and poor role modeling may contribute to the aggressive student's behavior. This category is divided into three subtypes; the difference is in the intensity of the aggression and the way the aggression is directed.

The *aggressive-hostile* student exhibits behavior and affect that are similar to the DSM IV diagnosis of conduct disorder. The symptoms for conduct disorder range from poor control over anger and impulses, difficulty empathizing with others, and an inability to see the consequences of one's actions to a sense of entitlement. These students take an inordinate amount of management time, which takes away from general study time.

The second type is *aggressive-oppositional*, which resembles the DSM IV diagnosis of oppositional-defiant disorder. This type of student is generally less destructive to property and people, but disrupts by arguing with adults, resisting rules, and being verbally harsh and critical of others. Students of this type tend to blame others for their problems.

The third type is *aggressive-covert*. This type is less destructive than the aggressive-oppositional student and does not as markedly exhibit the symptoms of a DSM IV classification. Students of this type tend to create disruptions that are less direct than those created by the first two types and more "behind the scenes." Nonetheless, these students seem to provoke conflicts among others. Because they are not as easy to spot as the other aggressive types, these students often avoid discipline for their behavior.

Although aggressive students do more than try their teachers' patience, firmness not anger, positive attention whenever possible, and creativity can help to turn their behavior around. The individual teacher's efforts may not be enough, however. Comprehensive management and discipline for this group involves a solid plan and structure created and implemented by the student's parents, school administrators, and the students themselves. Community services in the form of medication, psychotherapy, and group or family therapy may be useful. Programs such as Outward Bound can enhance students' knowledge of themselves and others. This combination offers the best opportunity to help these students learn to manage their own behavior as best they can.

Case Study

Howard is the terror of the high school. Although he is at least average in intelligence, he is very disruptive, and teachers suspect he bullies others outside of the school grounds. Miss Leah decides to take on the challenge. Based on her conversations with a social worker, she knows that Howard has problems at home and that his father is reportedly an alcoholic. She also knows that the community may need to be called in to assist Howard. Her conversation with Howard might go something like this:

> "Howard, I know that you are having a very hard time in school, and you are much brighter than that. I want to know what you think is the problem."

> "I don't give a blankety-blank-blank."

> "Howard, I am not against you at all, but I think you need more help. I'd like to call your parents to come in and talk. . . ."

> "Oh no, don't call my father. He'll kill me. Please, just my mom."

> "I'll do my best. I'll talk to other staff and see what we can do about that. We need to set up some rewards and consequences at home and at school to motivate you to do better in your schoolwork and with other students."

> "What do you mean?"

> "From now until the meeting, think of two things you really like, within reason, and two things you really don't like. We'll use that to set up a system that you, your mom, and the school can live with."

> "Sounds weird, but OK. Are you sure—two things I like?"

> "Yes, Howard, two things you like."

Miss Leah proceeds to schedule a meeting with all concerned.

Students with Attention Problems

Another group of high-needs students consists of children or adolescents with attention problems that are like the formal medical diagnosis of attention deficit disorder, either hyperactive or inattentive. This group has been in the public view recently because of controversies regarding misdiagnosis, overdiagnosis, and the use of medications. However, it appears likely that this group is an undertreated population (see, for example, the study conducted by Rowland et al., 2002, reporting that national estimates of children or adolescents with ADHD may be outdated).

Students who exhibit attention problems of the hyperactive type are most noted for their difficulty staying seated and taking turns, for interrupting others, and for poor impulse control.

Students of the second type, inattentive, are harder to spot because they may not draw attention to themselves but struggle to stay focused and are forgetful, disorganized, and often anxious.

Help for these students includes teaching organization and planning skills in more depth than other students commonly require. For both types, however, when the student is properly diagnosed, psychologists have found that medication can be helpful. It is useful for the teacher to realize that these students did not choose this problem, but they are responsible for working within the issue and learning the added skills they will need to be successful.

Case Study

Jason is, frankly, all over the place at once. He transferred from another school that did not seem to have a handle on his ADHD (which was noted in his school records). Miss Franklin, Jason's teacher, tackles the problem immediately by setting up a meeting with Jason and his parents to ask for their help:

"I'd like to start the meeting off with you, Mr. and Mrs. Anderson. What is your concern with Jason?"

"Well, Jason was diagnosed with ADHD and prescribed medication, but we don't feel comfortable with that. So we have tried a few things, like ADHD workbooks," Mrs. Anderson replies.

"I'm really glad to hear that. Maybe I could use some of those same ideas in the classroom."

"The skills that worked best were the schedule of assignments and saying self-calming statements to himself. He will do that sometimes."

Jason pipes in, "I forgot about all that stuff."

"You have already done a lot of work with this issue," Miss Franklin notes. "I think that the move may have been hard for him. I'll get that workbook and use the skills he is familiar with and then add from there. Does that sound good to the three of you?"

The Andersons agree.

"We appreciate that you are taking an extra interest in Jason," Mr. Anderson says. "This may work better than the last school."

"Thanks," says Jason.

Students Who Are Perfectionists

The category of perfectionist closely corresponds to the DSM IV diagnosis of obsessive-compulsive personality disorder. These students seem driven to succeed and propelled by multiple lists and expectations that take an inordinate amount of time to fulfill and that may lead to procrastination or abandonment of the project. Perfectionists need to be in control of how they and others perform tasks while appearing to be unaware of the effect of their behavior on others. Although some of these characteristics may seem worthy, the end result can be poor relationships and, in the worst case, depression and suicide. Conversely, some students who are perfectionists have given up on success because they cannot figure out how to do it perfectly, so they don't try at all.

Teachers can help these students by talking with them about the benefits of a positive attitude, focusing on improving relationships instead of simply focusing on their performance, and being flexible with themselves and others. It is also useful to let them know that it's OK to make mistakes—that that is how students learn. Mistakes will not lead to punishment in the classroom.

Case Study

Although Jessica is a model student, she never seems to take pleasure in what she accomplishes. There is always more to do or an extra-credit project to complete, and she does not have many friends. Mr. Haber decides to take some positives steps to stop Jessica's constant list making and negative self-attitude. He calls a meeting with her.

"What did I do wrong?" Jessica asks, before Mr. Haber has a chance to speak. "I thought I had an *A+* on that last exam."

"No, Jessica, you are doing fine; maybe *too* fine."

"That's a weird statement from a teacher!"

Mr. Haber continues: "Your school work, as you know, is at the top of the class, but you seem to take little joy in it and don't seem to want to be around your friends. Am I wrong?"

Jessica looks down. "I didn't think you noticed."

"I'd like to help balance things out a little better for you. How about helping some of the students who are more challenged than you are? You could help them and maybe make a friend too."

"Well . . . all right."

"And here's another idea: How about trying a little experiment? Make a small mistake outside of school on purpose and see how you feel about it. Then let's talk."

"Why? I could never do that!"

"Want to bet? I'll bet you 50 cents you can!"

"That's a deal! You are a strange one, Mr. Haber!"

Socially Inept Students

Socially inept students have difficulty making and keeping friends. They have not learned subtle physical and verbal cues that would enhance their relationships. Although they are well meaning, they annoy others by standing too close, speaking too loudly, or misreading others' comments, and they generally don't fit in. They often feel left out, sad, and different.

These students may need instruction on how to relate to others by using such common social courtesies as standing at an appropriate distance and being aware of the volume of their voice. This instruction may help eliminate or lessen the discomfort they feel. Teachers might refer to the book *Helping the Child Who Doesn't Fit In* (1992) by Stephen Nowicki and Marshall Duke for suggestions and background information.

Case Study

Bernardo stands out in a crowd. He's loud, goofy, and seems to annoy the other students. He is the target of jokes and pranks, mostly because of his name, his bowl haircut, and the very thick glasses he wears. He is a nice person but does not know how to interact with others without setting himself up for ridicule. Mrs. Cristofano wants to help him, and she wants a calmer classroom too.

"Bernardo, it seems as if you are having a hard time with the other students. Am I wrong?"

"No, that's right. I try hard but everybody laughs at me and hates my guts."

"Well, I am not so sure about that, but there is something we can do to help."

"Wow! Like what?"

"If you promise not to feel bad, I'll point some things out to you to help you blend in and get along better."

"Like what?" Bernardo is interested now.

"OK, here goes. How about talking a little softer and making sure you don't interrupt others?"

"I do that?"

"Yes, but you can fix that by really watching your behavior," Mrs. Cristofano replies.

"I think I can do that."

"And I will talk about bullying in class and also toughen up on those who make life hard for you. Maybe we should have a schoolwide announcement about that and let everyone know that bullying and mean teasing are not OK."

Bernardo's response is quick: "Boy, I'd like that!"

■ Section Reflection

Checking Your Understanding

Use the space provided to write your answers to the questions.

• Tom is a new student in your class who arrived during the fifth week of school. Now you are well under way with lessons, and many of the students have started to form friendships and bonds with one another. What strategies might you use to learn about Tom's interests, to integrate him into the class, and to help him develop relationships with other students?

• Over the past couple of days, three students who typically sit in the back of the room have been talking and goofing off during class. You know that one of the students, Eddie, has had a hard time making friends. You don't want to discourage the friendships that might be developing, but their behavior is distracting the class. What actions might you take?

- Regina is a new student in your class. You know that she was particularly close to her last teacher, but whenever you talk with her she seems withdrawn, even though you know she isn't normally shy. How might you deal with this situation?

- Max is usually willing to engage in any class discussion, but this week he isn't raising his hand and he isn't making eye contact with you. You recall that last week he gave several incorrect responses, and you may not have responded to those very well. What might you do to get Max re-engaged in the class?

- Lately you have received feedback from colleagues and from students that when someone is talking with you, you don't seem to be paying attention and don't seem to care what the other person has to say. What behaviors might you practice and adopt from those described for "Assertive Connector"?

A Self-Assessment

Circle the number on the scale that best matches your situation, with 0 indicating "Not at all" and 4 indicating "To a great extent."

I demonstrate that I am personally interested in students.

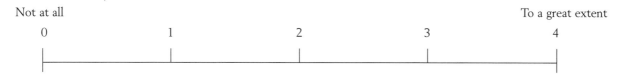

I use equitable classroom behavior.

My responses to students' incorrect answers validate students' participation and communicate that their answers are welcome and honored.

The way in which I communicate with students conveys that they are important and that I value what they say and do.

I have a commitment to learning about the needs of different types of students in my classes.

I am prepared to interact positively and productively with different types of high-needs students.

Not at all   To a great extent

0   1   2   3   4

4

MENTAL SET

Mental set is probably the aspect of classroom management that is least familiar to K–12 educators. As the name implies, it involves the mental readiness that a teacher brings to the management process. The importance of this factor might not be self-evident, but a little reflection validates its inclusion as an important part of classroom management.

Without an appropriate mental set, none of the other aspects of classroom management works very well. For example, a teacher might have spent a great deal of time establishing classroom rules and procedures. However, on a given day the teacher might be distracted by an incident in her personal life and fail to implement the rules and procedures she has established. Similarly, the teacher might have well-crafted disciplinary interventions. However, on a particular day she might be feeling irritable and fail to use those interventions, opting to vent her frustration by raising her voice to a student who has not followed a particular rule or procedure. In short, mental set deals with the ways a teacher thinks and behaves in the classroom moment to moment. The proper mental set facilitates all other aspects of classroom management.

This section includes two modules that address ways of thinking and behaving that constitute an effective mental set:

- Module 16: Exhibiting "Withitness"
- Module 17: Exhibiting Emotional Objectivity

■ Reflecting on Your Current Beliefs and Practices

Before reading the modules in this section, take some time to reflect on your beliefs and perspectives about the impact of a teacher's frame of mind on the functioning of the classroom. Then write your answers to the following questions in the space provided. Your responses will give you a basis for comparison as you read about the strategies recommended in these modules.

• In terms of classroom management, why is a teacher's mental set important?

• What are some behaviors you can adopt to ensure that you maintain a healthy and appropriate mental perspective?

• What strategies do you use to maintain or heighten your awareness of students' actions in the classroom and to notice and head off potential problems?

• Why do you think it is important to exhibit emotional objectivity toward students?

- What strategies do you use to ensure that you treat all students equitably, in spite of whatever thoughts about or reactions to particular students that you may have?

- What strategies do you use to prevent burnout?

- What do you do to recuperate when you feel overly tired, stressed, or on the verge of burnout?

- What strategies do you use to renew yourself after a stressful or otherwise negative interaction with a student or colleague?

Exhibiting "Withitness"

"Withitness" is a term coined by researcher Jacob Kounin (1970), who found that the most effective managers regularly monitor their classrooms and address even the possibility of misbehavior immediately. Withitness has been described in the following way:

> Effective managers monitored their classroom regularly. They positioned themselves so that they could see all students and they continuously scanned the room to keep track of what was going on, no matter what else they were doing at the time. (Good & Brophy, 2003, p. 112)

Recommendations for Classroom Practice

Four behaviors constitute withitness:

- Occupying the entire room
- Noticing potential problems
- Using a series of graduated actions
- Forecasting problems

Occupying the Entire Room

The first behavior associated with withitness is occupying the entire room, either physically or visually. Physically, you should spend relatively equal amounts of time in all quadrants of the classroom. This doesn't mean that it is inappropriate to spend the majority of time in the front of the room for a particular task,

project, or presentation. Standing or sitting in the front of the room is natural, for example, when you are presenting information using an overhead projector or PowerPoint.

However, when you are not presenting information, you should systematically walk to all areas of the room, paying particular attention to spots in the room that cannot easily be seen. Developing one or more patterns of movement is a good way to make sure that you "own" or occupy all parts of the room. One pattern might be to simply walk up one row and down another (assuming desks are arranged in rows). Another pattern might be to briefly stand in each quadrant of the room.

Even when you are standing still, you can attempt to include the entire class by making eye contact with every student. You can do this by making systematic sweeps of the class, trying to catch the gaze of every student. If a student is not willing to make eye contact, in fact, this may be an indication of potential misbehavior.

Noticing Potential Problems

Human nature leads us to ignore or avoid situations that pose the potential for trouble. If you are walking down the street and see two people in the beginning stages of an argument, you might tend to walk the other way. Nobody enjoys trouble. However, in the classroom, avoiding potential problems can actually encourage students to misbehave.

Noticing potential problems is simply a matter of being aware of student behavior that might serve as a warning sign. You should take note of the following signals:

• One or more students have not been engaged in class work for an extended period of time. For example, if a student or group of students has not answered any questions or raised a hand for a long time, this might indicate a potential problem.

• A group of students keep looking at one another and smiling.

• Members of the class are all looking at a specific part of the classroom.

• Students giggle or smile when you walk to a particular part of the classroom.

• When your back is turned, you repeatedly hear scuffling, whispering, or other noises from a specific part of the classroom.

Using a Series of Graduated Actions

Once you've noticed a potential problem, begin to take a graduated series of actions that more pointedly focus on the students in question. This series of actions might be summarized as follows:

• Look at the suspected students.

• Move in the direction of the students.

• Address the students in question; try to keep the incident from escalating.

• Stop the class and let everyone know that an intervention is required.

The first thing you might do is to simply look at the students who may cause a problem while remaining engaged with the academic content you're addressing. For example, you might answer a question from one student but look intently at two students in the back of the room who are engaged in some of the signal behaviors listed above. You would continue to answer the question but do so while looking intently at the students in question. You would not raise your voice, but your focused gaze should make it clear to all students that you're noticing something suspicious or inappropriate.

If the suspect behavior persists, the next step is to move in the direction of the troublesome students while continuing to look at them. When you are right next to them, stop and continue to address the class from this position. You should remain in this position until you are sure that the students in question are ready to engage in the classroom activity.

If students still have not joined in the classroom activity, then you should stop and address the student or students. Do this calmly but directly. You simply tell the students that you expect them to re-engage in the class. Again, you should do this calmly but with conviction. If possible, you should also do this quietly, so that only those students you are concerned about can hear the interaction. When addressing the students, it is useful to begin by saying something that might disarm them, such as, "I'm sure what you are doing is important to you, but I need you to pay attention to what we are doing" or "What we are doing in class right now is very important, and we need your participation. You can return to what you are doing after class is over." In short, your goal is to return the students' attention to class without allowing the incident to escalate.

Finally, if students are still not willing to engage in legitimate classroom activity, you should stop the class and announce that you will have to use one of the disciplinary interventions described in Section 2 of this handbook. However, you and the class, including the offending students, should be aware that the disciplinary intervention has been used as a last resort.

Forecasting Problems

The final aspect of withitness is forecasting problems. This occurs before students enter the classroom. You can forecast problems by mentally reviewing the students in class, noting any who are prone to misbehavior. For example,

you might note that two students in the next class have jointly and recently been involved in some behavioral incidents. You would simply make a mental note to pay particular attention to those students, perhaps meeting them at the door with a positive comment that puts them in a frame of mind conducive to learning. Such statements should not threaten students. Instead they should be invitations to participate in the class—for example, "Rodney and Mary, good to see you. I'm looking forward to a good lesson today."

In addition, you should note any incident outside of class that might stimulate misbehavior. For example, perhaps a student was involved in an argument at lunch with another student. Being aware of this, you might be particularly sensitive to that student during class, realizing that he or she is most likely upset and should be allowed time to calm down.

Exhibiting Emotional Objectivity

The title of this module is important to the understanding of this classroom management technique. Notice that the title is "Exhibiting Emotional Objectivity," not "Being Emotionally Objective." The distinction is subtle but important. It is virtually impossible to be emotionally objective about each student in your class. As human beings, we are emotional animals. We will have a natural affinity for some students but feel no affinity for others. Indeed, you might be naturally inclined to avoid some students in your classes.

Recommendations for Classroom Practice

The strategy of exhibiting emotional objectivity asks us to *behave* in an emotionally objective way even when we don't *feel* emotionally objective. This strategy has six elements:

- Recognizing that you are an emotional being
- Monitoring your thoughts and emotions
- Reframing
- Maintaining a cool exterior
- Taking care of yourself
- Preventing and recuperating from burnout

Recognizing That You Are an Emotional Being

To execute the strategy of emotional objectivity, it is important to realize that our feelings and thoughts frequently have little or nothing to do with reality and have no necessary relationship to our actions. We commonly react to people from the perspective of our past experiences and our beliefs about types of people. For example, you might have had an unpleasant experience with a person in your youth. Now, as a teacher, you encounter a student who reminds you of that person. Your negative emotional reaction has nothing to do with the student; it's simply a shadow from your past. Similarly, out of ignorance or lack of exposure, you might have formed a negative opinion about a certain type of person. When a student who exemplifies that type of person enters your class, you have a guarded or negative reaction.

These reactions are normal and part of the human condition. We all have preconceptions and prejudices that come from our past experiences, the way we were raised, and a variety of other factors. Feeling a certain way or thinking a certain way is understandable. However, we are accountable for how we act. Your thoughts and your feelings toward a particular student are not always attitudes that can be changed easily. However, how you *behave* toward that student is completely in your control. This concept provides great freedom for the classroom teacher. As human beings, we cannot be expected to have a natural affinity for every student in class. However, we *can* be expected to behave in a way that communicates care and concern for every student.

Monitoring Your Thoughts and Emotions

Although your actual behavior affects students more directly than your underlying feelings, it is important to be aware of those feelings and how you might consciously or unconsciously be harboring negative thoughts or emotions about certain students. Being aware of such students can help you treat them equitably. You can use the following steps to monitor your thoughts and emotions:

1. Mentally review the students in your class, noting your emotional reaction to each student.

2. For those students who arouse negative thoughts or emotions, spend some time trying to identify the specifics of your reactions. What specific negative *thoughts* do you have about those students? What specific negative *emotions* do you have about those students?

3. Try to identify events in your past that may be the source of your negative thoughts and emotions about those students.

To exemplify this process, consider a high school teacher who has reviewed the students in his class and determined that he has a fairly strong negative reaction to a young woman named Cassandra (Step 1). In Step 2, the teacher would spend some time thinking about the specifics of his reactions to Cassandra and perhaps make written notes for later reflection. The teacher might ask himself questions such as these:

- What specific thoughts am I having about Cassandra?
- Am I making negative judgments about her? What are they?
- What specific emotions do I feel when I think about her?

In Step 3, the teacher would think about things that have happened in the past that might be related to his negative reaction to Cassandra. He might ask himself questions such as these:

- Who or what does this student remind me of?
- Is there something that happened in the past that reminds me of the current situation? If so, how did I react in the past? What thoughts and emotions did I have about that experience?

Being more aware of the source of negative reactions to particular students can help lessen the hold that these reactions have on you and, therefore, help you treat those students equitably.

Reframing

Reframing refers to explaining a student's behavior in terms that are not threatening or offensive to you. Psychologist Ellen Langer

(1989) explains that people engage in reframing quite naturally in the normal course of life:

> . . . take a couple, Alice and Fred, whom you see quite often. Sometimes you hear them fight a bit. You don't pay any attention; don't all couples quarrel? Now you learn that they are getting a divorce. You call to mind all the evidence that explains this outcome. "I knew it; [I] remember how they used to fight. Their fights were vicious." On the other hand, perhaps you hear that they just celebrated their silver anniversary. "Isn't this nice," you say, "they have such a solid marriage; they hardly ever quarrel and when they do they always make up so sweetly to each other." (p. 64)

Although reframing occurs unconsciously and automatically in daily life, it is useful to do it consciously with students who arouse negative reactions. To do so, you would simply explain a student's negative behavior in a way that portrays the student in a more positive light.

To illustrate, assume that a teacher has had negative experiences with a particular student named Neal. The teacher has personalized these behaviors as actions intended to be disrespectful to him or to purposely arouse his anger. However, the student's behavior could have many other explanations. For example, Neal might be upset about an argument he had with a friend or family member, or he might be disappointed about something—perhaps he wasn't chosen for the football team or a friend he invited to a movie or activity turned him down. Perhaps something upsetting has been going on in Neal's personal life that the teacher isn't aware of, or perhaps Neal has a low sense of self-esteem. Viewing a student's actions in a way that gives the student the benefit of the doubt or helps you to feel compassion for the student can help provide some distance and, therefore, an opportunity for clearer thinking and more productive interactions.

Maintaining a Cool Exterior

Ultimately, emotional objectivity must be displayed through behavior in the classroom. A cardinal rule of emotional objectivity is that the teacher's demeanor in class should avoid extremes. This is particularly important for the emotion of anger. That is, even when you become extremely agitated with a particular student, you should not demonstrate the emotion nonverbally. Specifically, you should avoid aggressive nonverbal behaviors such as the following:

• Pointing a finger at the student or shaking your fist at the student
• Raising your voice as you speak
• Squinting your eyes
• Moving toward or hovering over the student

Instead, emotional objectivity involves exhibiting *assertive* behaviors such as the following:

• Speaking directly to the student in a calm and respectful tone
• Looking directly at the student, without glaring or staring
• Maintaining an appropriate distance from the student
• Being conscious of the look on your face—keeping your facial expressions neutral

Although it is not useful to express anger nonverbally, it is legitimate and even useful to express anger to students verbally. Again, however, this should be done in specific ways, including the following:

- Stating what, specifically, you are angry about without dramatizing or overemphasizing your reaction
- Using a calm and even tone of voice

Another strategy for maintaining a cool exterior is to use active listening and speaking. Researcher Howard Markman and his colleagues (Gottman, Notarius, Gonso, & Markman, 1976; Notarius & Markman, 1993) have studied the way people interact when they disagree or argue. The way we handle disagreements and arguments provides the groundwork for our future interactions with others. If we handle disagreements and arguments poorly, it is more likely that we will have negative interactions with others in the future. Conversely, if we handle disagreements and arguments well, we increase the probability of positive interactions in the future. We refer to the skill of handling an argument or disagreement well as "active listening and speaking." Before using this strategy with students in the classroom, it is useful to understand the basic concepts underlying active listening and speaking and to practice these skills with an adult.

The typical purpose of a communication is to transfer information from one person, the speaker, to another person or to a group, the listener or listeners. The speaker's information includes the content of the message; requests, if any; and the feelings of the speaker. Presumably, what the speaker is saying is important to the speaker, and he or she wants the listener to receive all of the information in the

communication. However, the speaker cannot know with certainty if the listener has heard the communication unless the listener can repeat the information, including the speaker's feelings. Active listening and speaking ensures that the listener has "heard" the speaker's communication. Figure 17.1 provides a structured way to practice active listening and speaking.

In the classroom, you probably will not be dealing with students who have practiced active listening and speaking. For these instances, we suggest the process described in Figure 17.2. Note that this figure includes two options. The first option is more passive than the second but requires less skill and practice to use effectively.

Active listening and speaking is a skill that takes time to develop, so it might require some effort on your part to feel comfortable with the strategies involved. However, we believe that the payoff in terms of classroom management is worth the effort. Remember that students are people who want to be heard, just like the rest of us. Although the listening and speaking process—like many of the processes in this handbook—may seem to take a long time, you will save time in the long run by demonstrating that you care and that you listen—while still conveying the message that you are in charge of the classroom environment.

Taking Care of Yourself

Perhaps the most important strategy for maintaining a healthy frame of mind is taking care of yourself. This is particularly true when you have had a negative encounter with students.

Even highly skilled classroom managers will occasionally have incidents that turn negative.

Figure 17.1
An Exercise in Active Listening and Speaking

To practice active speaking and listening, find a willing partner and use topics that don't have too much of an emotional overtone for either of you.

1. Have one person be the speaker and one be the listener. Stay in those roles until you both decide to switch. To help keep track of the roles, place an object, such as a box of tissues, in front of the person who is the speaker.

2. The speaker says about three or four average-length sentences about where he or she stands and how he or she feels about a particular topic. Only "I" statements should be used; for instance, say, "I feel angry that I didn't get my project done," as opposed to, "I think you caused me to not complete my project." "I" statements let the listener know how the speaker experiences his or her life. Such statements are more valuable than expressing the speaker's assessment of what the listener's thoughts, feelings, or opinions may be.

3. After these three or four sentences, the listener paraphrases back to the speaker what the listener heard—for instance, "What I heard you say is that you didn't get your project done and that you are feeling angry about that." If the listener is confused about what the speaker said, the listener may ask a simple question. At this step in the exercise, the listener should not add his or her own opinions, insights, or reactions to what the speaker said. To hear the speaker, the listener must stop the internal dialogue and potential rebuttals forming in his or her own mind and pay full attention to the speaker. This is harder to do than we might think!

4. The speaker decides whether the listener was accurate or not. If not, the speaker gently, calmly, and directly restates what he or she said until the listener can paraphrase it accurately, including the feelings of the speaker.

5. The speaker can continue until he or she feels that the communication is complete for the moment. This usually requires about four to five exchanges. Then the switch is made—the speaker is now the listener and vice versa. The speaker and the listener may need to change roles many times in order to complete a topic. Time spent in each role should be equal.

Remember, as the listener, you cannot express *any* of your own ideas. This disrupts the speaker and conveys that you are not interested in that person. You will have your chance when you are the speaker. Notice how hard it is to just listen to another person. You do not have to agree with the speaker to be a good listener.

At first, focus only on seeing each other's point of view before you attempt to solve the problem. You can't fix a problem if you don't know with accuracy what the problem is. You are more likely to come to a good solution and follow through on it if you have the experience of being heard and understood.

Figure 17.2

Active Listening and Speaking for Teachers—Interacting with Students

Option 1

1. As the student is speaking, simply listen without agreeing or disagreeing. Be as neutral as possible in your body posture, gestures, and facial expressions, but be actively focused on what the student is saying and try to completely understand the student's viewpoint.

2. When the student has finished speaking for the moment, just say, "I think I understand how you feel" or "I understand what you think." Then say, "What else is bothering you?"

3. Let the student speak again, and repeat the same process. After a while the student will not be able to think of anything else to say and will most likely be calmer, once he or she feels heard. To double-check, after the student appears to have finished speaking, ask the student one more time if there is anything else he or she wants to say. Most often, the student will say no. At this point, the student should be more able to hear what you have to say and will more likely go along with your requests.

Option 2

1. The primary listener (you, the teacher) takes the same approach as that described in Option 1; however, in addition, you should paraphrase what the student said. For example, instead of saying "I understand what you think," you should actually summarize what the student said. For instance, "You seem to be saying . . ." or "I understand that you feel or think . . . [paraphrase what the student said he or she felt or thought]."

2. It is useful at the end of your summary to ask, "Am I right?" or "Did I hear you completely?"

3. If you have accurately paraphrased what the student said, often the student will quickly say yes. If not, the student will correct you. At that point, restate what the student said the correction was. In other words, what the student is upset about is important to him or her; students will calm down when they feel that someone has taken the time to hear them out without distorting what they said or giving unsolicited opinions.

Although we stated previously that students' reactions to their teachers may have little to do with teachers themselves, negative incidents with students can have a dramatic effect on our mental state and our ability to interact effectively. Additionally, teachers' thoughts and feelings about situations in their personal and professional lives (such as marital troubles, health or financial concerns, or a disagreement with a colleague) frequently are reflected, even unwittingly, in interactions with students. No matter how hard we may try to keep feelings of sadness, upset, concern, or anger separated from our professional lives, these outside influences will affect our behavior as educators to some degree. It is unrealistic to expect otherwise. You may recall an occasion, for example, when you were aware that another teacher was going through a difficult time and you noticed a change in the teacher's behavior; if *you* noticed it, it's likely that the teacher's students did as well.

For these and other reasons, you will at times have negative encounters with your students. You may even act inappropriately toward a certain student. In such cases, the practice of taking care of yourself is particularly important.

As mentioned, negative encounters with students are a very common source of personal upset. One of the first things to do in such situations is to learn from the experience so that it is not repeated, but then to forgive yourself as you forgive students. Curwin and Mendler (1988) explain the reasons for this perspective:

> We have stated time and time again that it is critical for you not to carry anger, resentment, and other hostile feelings once a discipline situation is over. If you are angry with a student from an incident that happened the day before, you might encounter a power struggle just to flex your muscles and show who is boss. Don't. Start fresh each day. (p. 105)

The best way to ensure a fresh start is to do something that helps alleviate the negative emotions you feel. Toward this end, try one or more of the following activities.

Controlled Breathing. Sit in a comfortable chair and breathe calmly and evenly. Try to keep your mind free as you do so. You might set aside a few minutes over the lunch hour, at home before leaving for school, or at the end of the day. Find a private spot where you will not be disturbed by too much outside stimulation. As you breathe, simply focus on your breath.

Guided Imagery. Use guided imagery to create a "private retreat" for yourself that you

mentally visit for a few moments at the end of each day. This can be any situation that makes you feel calm and peaceful, such as lying on the beach, sitting at the base of a tree on a mountaintop, being inside your home by a fireplace, and so on. As with breathing exercises, you might set aside a few minutes at any appropriate point during the day to "visit" this mental retreat.

Funny Movies and TV Shows. Seek out movies and television shows that make you laugh. Laughter is one of the easiest and most effective ways to lessen the tension that accompanies an unpleasant experience. You might want to keep a copy of your favorite movie or television show on hand for just such times. In fact, just thinking about watching your favorite movie can help lighten the mood.

Special Treats. Be your own best friend by treating yourself to a reward on a particularly difficult day. Stop by your favorite coffee shop for a pastry or a latte, treat yourself to a whirlpool bath at the health club, make yourself a cup of your favorite hot tea, or sit in the sun and chat with a good friend. A reward like this can help balance the negative or unpleasant experience of the day.

Another surefire way to put everything into perspective is to *maintain a healthy sense of humor* about your encounters with specific students. For example, one teacher was having difficulty with a trio of disruptive 15-year-olds in his mathematics class. He decided that rather than getting upset regularly, he would try to lighten his own point of view. Once a week or so, he would write down run-ins he had with the boys and then watch his favorite Robin Williams comedy skit, trying to imagine what Williams would have said to them. Sometimes, the teacher actually came up with a funny line and tried it on the boys, and sometimes they'd even laugh! In any case, the teacher found a way to use humor to take care of himself. Another technique was employed by an entire middle school that was fortunate to have a gifted drama teacher. In addition to directing elaborate student productions like *Peter Pan*, the teacher also periodically collected groups of other faculty members to perform satirical skits at meetings. The groups were careful to avoid anything that resembled a personal attack and focused their creativity on situations and events that were common to the organization. All teachers agreed that the skits helped keep potentially annoying events in perspective.

Preventing and Recuperating from Burnout

A familiar term to most of us is *burnout*, an issue that is closely related to the strategy of taking care of yourself. Burnout is a popular distinction but not a therapeutic diagnosis. However, from the world of psychology to the world of business, burnout is associated with specific symptoms. Burnout may result from any number of issues outside or inside the classroom, such as an overly demanding schedule, extra responsibilities beyond teaching, too many students, or particularly challenging students or parents.

The list in Figure 17.3 may help you spot burnout in yourself and others. Figure 17.4 includes some ideas to help prevent or overcome burnout if you find that it is—or may become—a problem for you.

If these strategies don't help, you may be experiencing a deeper level of burnout worth

---

Figure 17.3
Characteristics of Burnout

- Depersonalization—feeling unreal, ungrounded, detached from oneself as if in a dream
- Reductions in personal accomplishment; forgetfulness; apathy
- Emotional exhaustion; increased physical illness, such as gastrointestinal problems; changes in appetite; sleep disturbances; strained eyes, back, and shoulders
- Quickness to anger; mood swings
- Increased "rigidity"; feeling overwhelmed
- Increased cynicism or negative self-talk
- Preoccupation with work, often to the exclusion of other aspects of life
- Changes in behavior, such as increased alcohol or drug use

---

exploring. Consider the mental health scale shown in Figure 17.5. Like most things in nature, such as height and weight, human mental health can be distributed along a bell curve.

On the lowest end of the scale is the category of *nonfunctional* people. These unfortunate folks have disabilities such as schizophrenia or major depression that are far beyond what most of us have experienced ourselves. Nonfunctional people are just that: they can't survive in the world without the help of others to care for at least some of their daily needs, be it medications, a safe place to live, food, clothing, financial aid, or the like. Sadly, many of these people do not get the help they sorely need.

Figure 17.4

Strategies for Preventing or Recovering from Burnout

- Use positive self-talk, such as "I can do this," "It will be over shortly," "Relax, breathe, I'm in control."

- Engage in some mild exercise—walk, swim, ride a bike.

- Practice good nutrition.

- Make time for yourself to read, meditate, or pray. Take a time-out.

- Set realistic goals; work smarter instead of harder.

- Create a laughter folder of good jokes; collect and watch comedy videos.

- Be around the most positive people you know; avoid negative people.

- Remember your purpose in teaching when you first started; recall the joy and excitement you once had.

The next group to consider is the *superior functioning* people on the highest end of the scale. This group includes some of our world leaders, such as Nelson Mandela and Mahatma Gandhi, and spiritual leaders, such as Mother Teresa. This group also includes many "ordinary" people who have mastered being human to the point where they can not only make contributions to their communities and families but also live their personal lives with love and integrity. For most of us, this is a goal we strive toward.

The next category is the *dysfunctional* level—that level right above the nonfunctional level. Although these people have more advantages than those in the nonfunctional category, their lives are fraught with problems. Some of the problems may stem from childhood abuse, neglect, untreated mental illnesses, or lack of well-developed life skills such as problem-solving strategies. As adults, some of these people have made poor life choices, such as abusing drugs or alcohol, not working hard enough to make an adequate living, or the like.

The next level to consider is the category of *average*. The people in this group often feel "OK" with their lives and are somewhat content but have a yearning for more. They may rationalize that their situation is the best they can expect from life but secretly hope they are wrong.

Between the categories of *average* and *superior functioning* is the category of *emotionally healthy*. These are people who *consistently* get things done, get along very well with others, and make a contribution to the lives of their family, friends, and coworkers. They are typically confident and at ease with who they are. They create few problems and are able to resolve the problems they encounter quickly and effectively. Their communications are clear and assertive.

One way to use this scale is to assess your own level of mental health, as outlined in Figure 17.6. Before doing so, it is important to realize that you probably exhibit behaviors from multiple categories. This is because throughout our lives, we are in one category at certain times but then move to another category later on. Additionally, we might exhibit the characteristics of different categories in different situations. You might notice, for example,

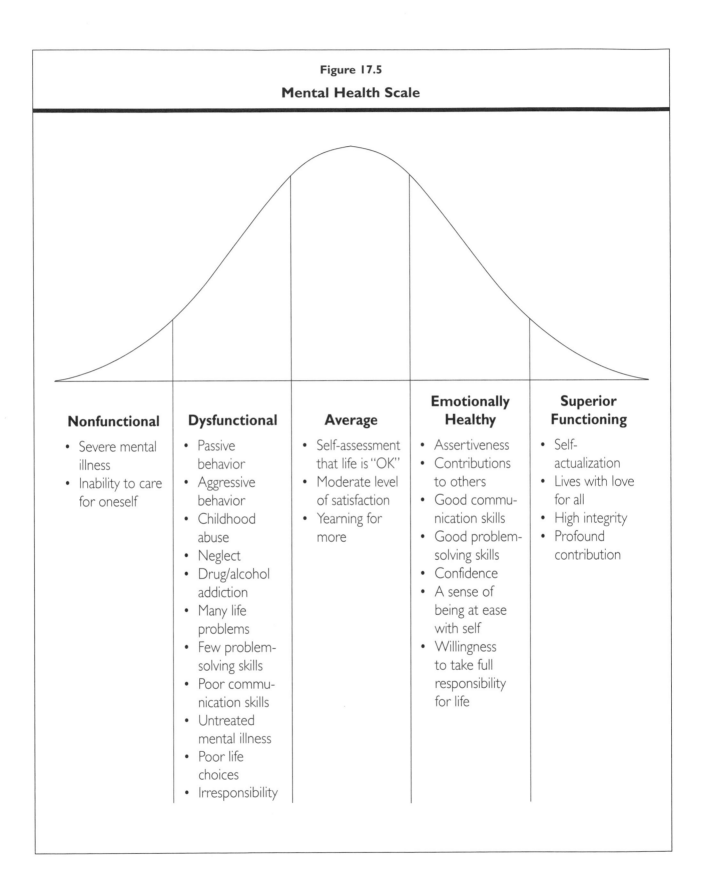

Figure 17.5

Mental Health Scale

Nonfunctional	Dysfunctional	Average	Emotionally Healthy	Superior Functioning
• Severe mental illness • Inability to care for oneself	• Passive behavior • Aggressive behavior • Childhood abuse • Neglect • Drug/alcohol addiction • Many life problems • Few problem-solving skills • Poor communication skills • Untreated mental illness • Poor life choices • Irresponsibility	• Self-assessment that life is "OK" • Moderate level of satisfaction • Yearning for more	• Assertiveness • Contributions to others • Good communication skills • Good problem-solving skills • Confidence • A sense of being at ease with self • Willingness to take full responsibility for life	• Self-actualization • Lives with love for all • High integrity • Profound contribution

---

Figure 17.6

Mental Health: An Assessment

Using the categories shown in Figure 17.5, rate the mental health level of the following:

- Yourself in general
- Your "family of origin"—your parents and siblings
- Your current home life
- The environment of your school
- Your relationships with your friends

If you have identified areas that are below the category of "Average," the next step might be to set goals for yourself regarding one or more of the following:

- Where you would generally like to be in terms of your mental health
- Where you would like to be in terms of your family of origin
- Where you would like to be in terms of your home life
- Where you would like your school to be
- Where you would like to be regarding your relationships with your friends

Although everyone, of course, strives to be in the mental health category of "Superior Functioning" in all aspects of their lives, this goal is probably quite optimistic. Setting a goal of being "Emotionally Healthy" in every area of your life is perhaps a more attainable goal.

---

that in school you have adopted many of the behaviors in the *emotionally healthy* category, but in some family situations you tend to adopt the behaviors in the *dysfunctional* category. Noticing this difference can lead to insights and, ultimately, to improvements in your viewpoint and actions.

In short, you can use this scale to gauge your mental health at a given time or in a given situation. You may be at a higher risk for burnout if your overall mental health is less than adequate. Identifying those things that would create the most positive changes in your life will have benefits that go far beyond the classroom.

■ Section Reflection

Checking Your Understanding

Use the space provided to write your answers to the questions.

- Your class is immersed in a project on whales. The groups have been working together intently and appropriately, and they appear to be having fun, too. But your "antennae are up" because one group's "fun" seems to be escalating, and you hear whale sounds coming from that part of the room. You don't want to squelch their enthusiasm, but you have the sense that their behavior could soon have a negative effect on everyone else. What are some strategies you might use?

- Luke, a student in your class, dresses in what you consider to be odd ways. You also notice that you have judgments about his hairstyle and how he walks. You are distracted by your reactions to Luke whenever he's around. But Luke is a good student. What strategies might you use to ensure that your internal, personal reactions to Luke aren't getting in the way of your ability to interact with him productively and be a good teacher to him?

- One of the students in your class, Sabrina, has refused to do her homework the past couple of days, and she has been whispering and goofing off in class. Over the lunch hour, you overhear her making a derogatory comment about you. Now you are really angry. You thought that she liked and respected you, but now you're not so sure. Based on what you learned from this section, what specific actions might you take? If you talk with Sabrina, what specific *aggressive*, nonverbal behaviors should you avoid? What specific *assertive* behaviors should you strive to use?

- Just as the day is ending, one of your students, Billy, says he needs to talk with you right away. He is upset that you have assigned homework over the weekend because a big football play-off game is scheduled, and he says he has "lots of other plans." How might you use the strategy of active listening and speaking in this situation?

- You are exhausted after weeks of evening parent-teacher conferences and late nights spent preparing students' report cards. It feels as though you don't have a spare minute to yourself. What should you do to take care of yourself, even when it seems that you have no time?

A Self-Assessment

Circle the number on the scale that best matches your situation, with 0 indicating "Not at all" and 4 indicating "To a great extent."

I regularly monitor my classroom and address behavioral issues before they are problems.

I exhibit emotional objectivity with all students, even when I have negative reactions or judgments toward certain students.

If I have a negative reaction to a student, I am effective in identifying the source of my reaction and reframing the issue.

When I have a disagreement with a student or a student is upset about something, I am effective in communicating in such a way that the student experiences being heard and is left feeling empowered.

I regularly monitor my mental and physical health.

I regularly draw on a number of strategies to take care of myself and ensure that I am able to work at my best level.

Not at all   To a great extent
    0   1   2   3   4

5

STUDENT RESPONSIBILITY

The actions a teacher can and should take regarding classroom management are numerous. From setting the right tone to taking the lead in setting rules and consequences, the teacher is the guiding force in the classroom. But students, too, play a role in how well-managed the classroom is. For example, when students come to class prepared, turn in their work on time, and resolve conflicts with their peers, they help make the learning environment more productive and satisfying. In fact, the attitude and practice of taking personal responsibility for one's actions is one of the most important factors contributing to overall student productivity, grade point average, and personal satisfaction.

Self-responsibility has many dimensions and associated terms, including *self-discipline, self-management, self-regulation, self-control,* and *social skills*. The common theme is the focus on developing and strengthening aspects of one's self.

Although ample evidence suggests that teaching students to be responsible for themselves is a high priority for parents, educators, and community members alike, many teachers don't focus on this aspect of classroom management. As discussed more fully in *Classroom Management That Works* (Marzano, 2003), cultivating these attitudes and behaviors in students requires more of teachers than other classroom management issues. First, it takes time. Second, it requires developing a different type of relationship than the type teachers typically have with their students and with students' parents and guardians. For these reasons, many people fail to identify student responsibility as one of the key elements of effective classroom management. However, we strongly recommend that teachers take this on, given the significant and likely long-term payoffs.

Teaching students to be responsible for themselves can begin in the earliest grades. Even very young children can learn to be responsible for themselves, to recognize others' feelings and perspectives, and to respond empathetically to others. Teaching responsibility and self-management is even more important for students with behavioral problems. Arming students with these skills increases their ability not only to resolve conflicts but also to prevent conflicts before they arise, leading to a healthier classroom and to students who are better prepared to be good community members. Though many teachers shy away from this area because of the time involved, in the long run, helping students develop the skills of personal responsibility will actually save time because fewer classroom disruptions and conflicts will occur.

This section covers three broad topics for teaching and enhancing student responsibility and thereby improving the overall management and effectiveness of the classroom:

- Module 18: The Nature of Responsibility
- Module 19: Strategies for Personal Development
- Module 20: Strategies for Conflict Prevention and Resolution

■ Reflecting on Your Current Beliefs and Practices

Before reading the modules in this section, take some time to reflect on your beliefs and perspectives about student responsibility and any current practices you follow in the classroom. Then write your answers to the following questions in the space provided. Your responses will give you a basis for comparison as you read about the strategies recommended in these modules.

- In terms of classroom management, why might it be useful to teach students about personal responsibility?

- How might teaching students about personal responsibility benefit them in the long run?

- What are some specific situations in which it would help students if they were more responsible for themselves?

- Do you currently teach students any type of self-responsibility strategies? If so, what strategies do you teach? How effective has your approach been?

- What procedures and structures do you currently use in the classroom to prevent and resolve conflict?

- What are the benefits of using these approaches?

- What has worked about the approaches you've used? What hasn't worked?

- What questions or concerns do you have about using class time for activities such as these?

The Nature of Responsibility

What does it mean to be "responsible" for ourselves? From one perspective, it means that if something goes wrong, we are to blame; if something goes right, we are to be applauded. A different, perhaps more empowering view of responsibility is that it simply means acknowledging that we are the cause of many of our thoughts, emotions, and actions; how we affect others; and some of our life situations. There's something useful to be gained by considering that we are responsible for these things. A third view is that "taking responsibility" involves objectively stating the facts of a situation without a negatively oriented attempt to determine who was to blame or who was at fault. When we can simply see the facts of a situation and acknowledge our appropriate share of creating that situation, it is easier to see suitable solutions and appropriate actions to take. This third perspective is the one we recommend for the classroom, although the others have their merits.

It is important to emphasize two points before introducing students to this view of responsibility. First, the definition and description of responsibility should not be used to make students feel ashamed or disempowered in any way, but rather to empower them to do as well as they possibly can. In particular, this view of responsibility does *not* include a student's assuming responsibility for abusive or inappropriate behavior or treatment by anyone in their lives. At times a student may be a victim of crime or violence; verbal, sexual, or physical abuse; harassment; taunting; or other acts that anyone would find illegal or unacceptable. In these situations, the student, along with his or her parents or guardians, should be supported in seeking whatever help is needed to deal with the situation.

The second point is that the concept of personal responsibility should be used to help students in areas that they truly have control over or can change. There are some behaviors or situations that students simply cannot change or cannot change without help. For instance, a student may have great difficulty giving a speech if he has an anxiety disorder or ADHD but has not received appropriate medical or psychological attention and has not learned to use coping strategies. In an anxiety-producing situation, this student may have an impossible task ahead of him, through no fault of his own.

Therefore, we recommend that you address the concepts presented in this section with great care. In particular, you should be mindful of signs that students are misusing these concepts, blaming themselves for someone else's inappropriate behavior, feeling overwhelmed at their inability to change their own or another's behavior, or assuming blame for a medical or psychological condition that has not been addressed adequately. In addition, it is useful to remember how difficult it is at times to change your own behavior and that students may have an even tougher time doing so.

Recommendations for Classroom Practice

You can teach students about the nature of responsibility in a number of ways. In this module, we discuss the following strategies to use in the classroom:

- Helping students understand what responsibility is—and is not
- Helping students understand the difference between facts and interpretations

Helping Students Understand What Responsibility Is—and Is Not

A useful place to start teaching about personal responsibility is to offer a definition and description of *responsibility* for students to react to and discuss. Figures 18.1 and 18.2 present two examples of definitions and descriptions of responsibility—one for younger (elementary-level) students and one for older (secondary-level) students. Regardless of how old students are, it is useful to talk with them about responsibility using the information in Figures 18.1 and 18.2 as background; or, if appropriate, you might directly share this information with students. You might post a description of or basic points about responsibility somewhere in the room or prepare a handout that students can put in a notebook.

The point of asking students to consider adopting the view of responsibility depicted in Figures 18.1 and 18.2 is to help enhance their understanding of the nature of responsibility so that they may be more responsible. Like the rest of us, students will not simply read these descriptions, say "Wow! That sounds great!" and suddenly become completely responsible for their actions. Learning to become responsible takes time and a great deal of practice.

In light of this, it is useful to introduce students to some basic terms related to responsibility. These terms should be explained, discussed, and then informally defined as in Figure 18.3. Equally important, you should use the terms consistently to describe and discuss classroom behavior.

One way to reinforce the language of responsibility is to use it to describe characters in literature or people in the news who demonstrate taking responsibility for their actions, in both positive and negative situations. Another way to help students better understand responsibility is to ask them to complete the exercise in Figure 18.4. These situations are offered as examples to stimulate discussion. You and your students might brainstorm other situations that relate to the classroom, classmates, or yourselves.

Helping Students Understand the Difference Between Facts and Interpretations

Understanding the concept of responsibility requires making an important distinction—namely, the distinction between interpretations and facts. You might share the examples in Figure 18.5 with students to jump-start a conversation about this distinction and how it applies

Figure 18.1

Responsibility: A Description for Younger Students

When we hear the word *responsibility,* we often think that it means we are wrong or bad. Maybe we have been told that if we say we're responsible, we'll get in trouble. But being responsible is very different from that! Being responsible means saying what happened and saying how we contributed to what happened.

Being responsible begins by stating the facts of a situation as if a video camera were taking pictures of what's going on. Then we can more accurately see what part *we* played in a problem or in a successful experience. It doesn't mean that others had nothing to do with what happened. It simply means that it's useful to *first* see what we did and what we didn't do.

If there was a problem and we have some responsibility for what happened, we can apologize, fix the situation if appropriate, and not do it again. Or if the situation is one in which we did something well, we can learn what worked and apply that to other situations. That's all that *responsibility* means.

Responsibility involves these three steps:
1. Pretend that a video camera is recording the situation. Look at what the facts are as the camera sees them.
2. Decide what part you played in the problem or the successful situation. It's okay if you made a mistake! And it's okay to say if you did something great.
3. If you did have responsibility for something that was not good, take positive action to correct the situation as much as possible, such as apologizing, fixing the problem, or promising not to do it again and then not doing it again! If the situation involves something you did well, take the time to acknowledge your success.

Responsibility is not . . .
- Looking at the situation from your viewpoint only (for instance, focusing on what the other person did wrong).
- Interpreting the situation in a way that makes you seem a certain way (for instance, innocent or overly guilty) rather than sticking to the facts.
- Waiting for the other person to solve the problem if you have responsibility for it.
- Allowing other people to take credit for what you accomplished.

Think about what it would be like if everyone took 100 percent responsibility for the problems and successes they created. Wouldn't that be great?

Important: Responsibility is *not* thinking you are to blame if someone verbally or physically abuses you, or does something else that is clearly wrong. If at any time you aren't completely sure, talk to your parents, your teacher, or your guidance counselor.

Figure 18.2

Responsibility: A Description for Older Students

Many students as well as many adults have difficulty taking responsibility for the positive and negative situations that happen in their lives. If we have accomplished something positive and received acknowledgment from others, we may feel embarrassed or shy. If we have done something negative, we may fear punishment and humiliation, especially if that's how someone reacted to us in the past.

Taking responsibility means simply stating the facts as they are—not interpreting what happened—and then correcting the situation if you created a problem, or acknowledging a success if you accomplished something. A simple way to think about taking responsibility is, "I did what I did, and I didn't do what I didn't do." Correcting a negative situation can mean many things. For example, we might apologize for our actions or acknowledge what we said or did (or didn't say or do) that contributed to the situation, take action to fix the problem, and promise not to do it again. If you accomplished a goal, then allow others to praise or reward you.

When we are responsible for our behavior, we gain the respect of others and ourselves. The more mature we are, the more willing we are to take responsibility for our behavior and our lives. Being responsible for ourselves is a choice.

Look at the graph below. Many people function as if they are innocent until proven guilty rather than being very honest and thoughtfully looking at their own behavior first. It is more personally powerful to look at the situation as if you alone created the entire situation, and then to lower your level of responsibility only if that isn't true.

0% - 100%

No responsibility/"victim"   Personal responsibility

People usually say this: *Instead, try saying these things:*

"It's not my fault. They did it!"   "I'm responsible until I prove otherwise."

                                                       "I might have had something to do with what happened."

                                                       "I'll look carefully to see if I had a part in this."

Being personally responsible for situations gives us a powerful position from which to create the life we want without making excuses, blaming others, or living as a helpless victim.

Figure 18.3

The Language of Responsibility

Taking responsibility—accurately assessing any and all accountability that you may have in a situation

Blaming someone else—assuming that someone else is responsible before assessing your own responsibility

True victim—the actual recipient of abuse, criminal activity, or neglect

False victim—someone who pretends to be a true victim despite actually having responsibility in the matter

Facts—what could be proven in a court of law, what a video camera would record; data without interpretations

Interpretations—a point of view that adds a slant or spin to the facts

Self-empowerment—thoughts and behaviors that promote one's well-being and productivity and create positive feelings in relationships

Self-disempowerment—thoughts and behaviors that decrease one's well-being and productivity and create negativity in relationships

Empowering someone else—behaving and speaking to another in ways that help the person create more well-being, productivity, and positive relationships

Disempowering someone else—behaving and speaking to another in ways that harm the person's well-being, productivity, and relationships

Consequences—the natural outcomes of poor behavior, attitudes, and communication

Benefits/rewards—the natural outcomes of positive behavior, attitudes, and communication

Being right—assuming you are right and someone else is wrong without first taking responsibility for your part

Making someone else wrong—similar to blaming someone else but, in addition, trying to make the person feel guilty, humiliated, or bad about himself or herself; attacking someone else's self-worth and believing or saying that the person is less worthy than you are

Figure 18.4

Exercise to Introduce Responsibility

Whose responsibility is it?

	My Responsibility	The Other Person's Responsibility	The Teacher's or Another Adult's Responsibility	Everyone's Responsibility
Completing my homework				
My friend completing his or her homework				
Keeping the school building clean				
A fight on the playground				
Someone hitting me				
Me hitting someone				
Keeping my supplies organized				
Acting appropriately in spite of how others are acting				
Someone cheating on his or her schoolwork				
Forgetting my lunch money				
A friend forgetting his or her lunch money				
Keeping my hands and feet to myself				
Talking in class while the teacher is talking				
Being kind to others				
Stopping gossip about others				

Figure 18.5

Facts vs. Interpretations or Judgments

Statements of Fact

Sue walked over to the group and put her books on the table we were sharing. Then she said, "I don't want to work with you." Peter said, "What's your problem?" Sue said, "I just don't feel like working on this."

Statements of Interpretation/Judgment

Sue walked over to the group in a big huff and threw her books on the table we were sharing. Then she yelled, "I don't want to work with you." She was a real jerk. Peter snarled, "What's your problem?" Sue said in a really mean way, "I just don't feel like working on this."

Statements of Fact

David was playing on the jungle gym, hanging by one arm. Erica climbed up the jungle gym. She seemed to bump into David, and he fell to the ground. David held his arm and started to cry.

Statements of Interpretation/Judgment

David was playing on the jungle gym, hanging by one arm. All of a sudden, Erica jumped on the jungle gym and shoved past everyone. She deliberately pushed David, and he fell to the ground. David grabbed his arm and started to cry. Now, all because of Erica, David's arm is messed up.

---

to situations they have faced, or might face, in school and in life. You might also seek out examples from stories in history or literature in which people or characters interpreted what happened in ways that differed from what actually happened.

Being able to state the facts can be particularly useful in "calming the waters" in an emotionally charged situation. Sometimes the reason we get upset is because we negatively interpret something that happened and think that our interpretation is the "truth." Our "slant" or "spin" about what happened can add a layer of judgment about ourselves or others onto an event. To explore this idea further, you might ask students to try the exercise in Figure 18.6. After students complete the exercise, you can lead a discussion about how they think they might feel after each interpretation, how others might respond to someone who is interpreting a situation in a certain way, which interpretation they have preferred in the past, which one they wish others would use, and which one they'd like to use in the future.

Note that the first four interpretations ("tragic," "paranoid," "guilt-ridden," and "blaming") generally lead to negative emotions, poorer outcomes, and lower self-esteem. The "funny" interpretation tends to lighten the mood. The "practical" interpretation is mostly a restatement of the facts; and the "enlightened" interpretation (which is perhaps more forward-looking) reflects a deeper meaning and encourages finding something positive about the situation.

Figure 18.6

Facts vs. Interpretations: An Exercise

The following exercise may be used as class discussion or journal material using various topics such as recent world events or a piece of literature. Students might also try the exercise using a personal issue in their lives, such as something that slightly annoyed them.

Examples:
- *World events:* A recent outbreak of mad cow disease.
- *Literature:* In Robert Peck's novel *A Day No Pigs Would Die,* the main character is a young boy who has a pet pig.
- *An individual student's life situation:* I got a C on my math test.

Have students first list the facts about an event and then generate a number of possible interpretations. An example of the facts surrounding the individual student's life situation follows along with a number of interpretations.

The Facts: I was studying and my brother played his music loudly. I asked him to stop and he didn't. The next day I got a C on my math test.

Interpretations:
- Tragic—It is horrible that this happened. Now I'll never get into college!
- Paranoid—My stupid brother is trying to make me fail.
- Guilt-ridden—It happened because I made fun of his music and I am being paid back.
- Blaming—If my brother wasn't such a jerk, this never would have happened.
- Funny—If he had played hip hop music instead, I would have gotten an A. (Note: comedians do this with many different topics, be creative!)
- Practical—I got a C, so I'll have to try harder next time. No excuses!
- Enlightened—Maybe this happened for a reason, and I can learn something from this.

Present students with this example (or one you have devised), moving from the facts only to various interpretations. Then have students try this on their own with an issue that is important to them.

Identify something that has happened to you that has caused you mild annoyance and write out the facts as if a video camera had recorded it.

_____

_____

(continued)

Figure 18.6

Facts vs. Interpretations: An Exercise (continued)

Make up an interpretation that is

Tragic: _____

Paranoid: _____

Guilt-ridden: _____

Blaming: _____

Funny: _____

Practical: _____

Enlightened: _____

Once you have generated your interpretations, identify which interpretation is the most accurate:

_____

_____

What is your evidence that it is the most accurate interpretation?

_____

_____

Which interpretation makes you feel the most empowered? Why?

_____

_____

_____

Which interpretation makes you feel the least empowered? Why?

_____

_____

_____

What are some awarenesses you have gained from doing this exercise?

_____

_____

Module 19

Strategies for Personal Development

In addition to teaching students about the nature of responsibility, you can introduce and then reinforce specific strategies throughout the school year to help them take more responsibility for their actions. Decisions about how and when to introduce these strategies and the degree to which you should reinforce them depend on students' age and maturity. Of course, you also must be highly sensitive to the dispositions of individual students in terms of how they may react to specific ideas being introduced in the class and use good judgment about the strategies that are appropriate for your students.

Recommendations for Classroom Practice

Quite a few strategies can help students develop their sense of personal responsibility. In this module, we highlight three:

- Helping students develop self-awareness
- Teaching students the strategy of positive self-talk
- Teaching students how to be assertive

Helping Students Develop Self-Awareness

The foundation of developing personal responsibility is the act of becoming more and more self-aware. As adults, increasing self-awareness includes learning to notice our thoughts, our emotions, our behaviors, and the impact of these on ourselves and others. The more self-aware we are, the more we can begin to be responsible for ourselves and our lives. The same can be said for students. Even very young students can benefit from beginning to develop self-awareness.

To fully understand ourselves, we must understand our emotions. Every human being experiences the same emotions, regardless of the culture he or she was born into. According to researcher Steven Pinker (1997), sociologists have mistakenly concluded that people from some cultures do not experience certain emotions, but this observation fails to take into account our shared humanity:

> Cultures surely differ in how often their members express, talk about, and act on various emotions. But that says nothing about what their people feel. The evidence suggests that the emotions of all normal members of our species are played on the same keyboard. (p. 365)

Reflecting on Pinker's statement, Marzano (1998) explains:

> The keyboard Pinker refers to is the internal physiological states produced by the limbic system. Stated differently, all cultures experience the same range of physiological states or feelings. However,

the extent to which they have names for these states or openly discuss these states differs dramatically from culture to culture. (p. 25)

Human beings not only experience the same emotions, but they tend to express them in similar ways. More than 130 years ago, Charles Darwin discussed the commonality in emotional expression, especially facial expressions, among peoples around the world in *The Expression of the Emotions in Man and Animals* (1872):

> The same state of mind is expressed throughout the world with remarkable uniformity, and this fact is in itself interesting as evidence of the close similarity in bodily structure and mental disposition of all races of mankind. (p. 18)

Darwin noted that the similarity in emotional expression is the same among people of widely diverse racial and cultural backgrounds and even among those born blind, lending weight to his statement that our shared emotional expressions are "innate and inherited, that is, have not been learnt by the individual" (p. 352).

Building on these ideas and on the work of numerous researchers, including Silvan Tomkins, Carroll Izard, Paul Ekman, Robert Plutchik, and Nico Frijda, we have identified six basic emotions, which are listed in Figure 19.1. This figure also includes, for each emotion, brief notes about facial expressions, body posture, gestures, and so on that might be associated with the emotion. The information in this figure may be useful as background information for a discussion of emotions and as guidance to help some students understand why they are misinterpreted by others. For instance, if a student tends to scowl even when

he is not feeling angry, other students might rightfully think of the student as "always mad." Similarly, if a student appears relaxed and is laughing (glad), but is speaking about a loss or disappointment (sad), others might rightfully be confused or may assume that the student doesn't care about her loss or disappointment.

It is important to stress that how people express their emotions can vary dramatically depending on their nationality or cultural or ethnic background. For instance, in some cultures, avoiding eye contact is a sign of respect, not a sign of avoidance, fear, or shame. To expand on this idea, you may wish to invite the class to create their own list of the ways in which eye contact, body posture, and other things might vary depending on one's family or nationality, culture, or ethnic background. Ideas for discussion might include how someone from one culture may react to the facial expressions of someone from another culture who is sad, for example. The overall intent of such an exercise is to give students some general guidelines for recognizing different emotions that they or others may be experiencing and to help them be sensitive to how cues for emotions may differ across cultures.

Teaching Students the Strategy of Positive Self-Talk

Our minds are the most powerful tools we have. They also are full of all types of thoughts, including opinions and judgments about ourselves, about others, and about things that have happened, might happen, or could happen. Thoughts may or may not be useful and productive. In fact, it might be said that our minds can be a friend or an enemy to us.

Figure 19.1
Emotional Expressions—Broad Descriptors

Glad

Eye contact—Frequent but not constant

Body posture—Relaxed

Facial expressions—Eyebrows in normal position or raised; smiling; mouth wide open in laughter

Gestures—Hands open, arms moving in a friendly manner (for example, open or raised during laughter)

Voice tone—Higher tone, loud or soft; laughter, chuckling

Verbal message—Inclusive, accepting of self and others, expressing positive statements

Sad

Eye contact—Eyes downturned, maybe crying

Body posture—May be leaning forward, shoulders slumped; rocking back and forth, legs squeezed together

Facial expressions—Mouth turned down at the corners; skin may be flushed or blotchy

Gestures—Hands at chest, stomach, or face; arms may be flailing or close to the body

Voice tone—Low to high volume

Verbal message—Speaking about losses, disappointments, missed opportunities, pain caused by others

Mad

Eye contact—Direct, prolonged stare

Body posture—Leaning forward, standing too close to someone else, legs in wide stance, trying to appear as large as possible; arms far from body

Facial expressions—Eyebrows pulled together, down in center; nostrils flared, lips pinched horizontally to show teeth

Gestures—Hands in fists, clenched and raised as if to strike; may hit and shove another; may point at other

Voice tone—Harsh, loud, intense; low-tone range; growling, shouting

Verbal message—Demanding, attacking, mocking, belittling, criticizing, threatening

Afraid

Eye contact—Darting, wide open; looking for escape routes

Body posture—Moving backward; hair erect; quivering; shallow breathing; heart racing; chest pulled in with shoulders forward, arms and legs pulled toward trunk; frozen in place or making jerking motions to escape

Facial expressions—Mouth turned down at corners or in "O" shape

Gestures—Hands at chest, arms grasping for balance

Voice tone—Quivering, unsteady, loud or soft

Verbal message—Submissive, pleading, false agreement

(continued)

Figure 19.1
Emotional Expressions—Broad Descriptors (continued)

Ashamed
Eye contact—Eyes averted
Body posture—Slumped forward; head down; slow breathing
Facial expressions—Eyebrows together in center; mouth turned down
Gestures—Hands together or arms limp at sides
Voice tone—Soft
Verbal message—Admission of guilt or error; negative self-talk; asking for forgiveness

Surprised
Eye contact—Eyes wide open
Body posture—Stepping back; head pulled back; shoulders up; sharp inhalation
Facial expressions—Mouth in "O" shape
Gestures—Arms moving to balance
Voice tone—Gasp, scream
Verbal message—Statement of fear or shock

At times it may seem as though we have no control over our minds, but we do. Over the past 50 years or so, psychologists have discovered that we can control our minds in some ways. Research has shown, for example, that positive self-talk improves the quality of our lives. In his ground-breaking book *Learned Optimism*, noted psychologist Martin Seligman (1990) states:

> Life inflicts the same setbacks and tragedies on the optimist and the pessimist (the positive and negative thinker), but the optimist weathers it better. The optimist bounces back from defeat, and, with his life somewhat poorer, he picks up and starts again. The pessimist gives up and falls into depression. Because of his resilience, the optimist achieves more at work, at school and on the playing field. The optimist has better physical health and may even live longer. Americans want optimists to lead them. Even when things go well for the pessimist, he is haunted by forebodings of catastrophe. (p. 207)

Great freedom and energy are available when we decide that we will control our thoughts instead of letting our thoughts control us. To this end, being aware of and controlling our self-talk is one of the most powerful things we can do. Figures 19.2 and 19.3 include exercises that you might use or adapt to help students understand the benefits of positive self-talk and learn how to develop this skill.

Teaching Students How to Be Assertive

Another exceptionally powerful concept for students and teachers alike is that of assertive behavior. Infants are born assertive; they cry when they are hungry, wet, or lonely.

Figure 19.2
Self-Talk Exercise for Younger Students

Part 1. Think about an event that happened this week that you felt good about. Do you notice that you had thoughts about the event, the other people involved, and how you felt? What were you saying to yourself? _____

_____

Were you saying good things or bad things about yourself and the other person? _____

_____

Do you agree with the idea that you were probably saying positive things about yourself and the other person? _____

Part 2. Now think of an event that happened this week that you felt bad about. What were you saying to yourself? _____

_____

_____

Were you saying good things or bad things about yourself and the other person? _____

Do you agree with the idea that you were probably thinking negative things about yourself and the other person? _____

Part 3. Think of an adult whom you like to be around. Write two or three reasons why you like this person. _____

_____

_____

Is this person a positive person or a negative person? _____

You probably like to be around adults and students who tend to be positive. People who are positive are generally more fun to be around and are more helpful, and they make you feel better about yourself.

(continued)

Figure 19.2

Self-Talk Exercise for Younger Students *(continued)*

Part 4. Think of words that go through your mind about yourself that sound negative. Write down the words. _____

Do you think these words are true? (They probably aren't!) _____

Do these words or thoughts make you feel better or worse? _____

What might happen if you decided to think a positive thought about yourself instead? _____

_____

Try to develop a positive thought about yourself. Write down that thought. _____

_____

Part 5. Try to think only positive thoughts for a day. How do you feel at the end of that day?

_____

_____

Caregivers and the immediate environment then either foster or squelch that assertiveness. As many successful people know, being passive, aggressive, or passive-aggressive is not productive. The only long-term workable behavior is assertive behavior. Learning to be assertive can take time, but the rewards are many: higher self-esteem, healthier relationships, and a greater sense of satisfaction and personal accomplishment.

The terms *passive, passive-aggressive, aggressive,* and *assertive,* as used to describe behavior, have been poorly defined in our culture, and they often are used casually and without specificity. Precise definitions of these four distinct concepts can be quite informative. Figure 19.4 includes basic definitions of these behaviors, which you might share with students or use

as background for classroom discussions and interactions.

As you review these definitions with students, it may be useful to stop after each one and ask students if they know anyone in literature, on TV, in sports, in the music industry, or in their personal lives who might fit the description of the behavior for each category. It is best to restrict students to identifying people outside the classroom and their peer groups to avoid hurt feelings. Most students will recognize that they tend to be attracted to assertive people, want to avoid aggressive people, are aggravated with passive-aggressive people, and like but don't necessary respect passive people.

As the class goes through the list, students may see themselves in primarily one category

---

Figure 19.3

Self-Talk Exercise for Older Students

We are with ourselves always—24 hours a day, 7 days a week. Whether we are aware of it or not, our minds are constantly going: giving us information, making judgments, and forming ideas. This has an enormous effect on how we feel about ourselves, others, and the rest of the world. Although this internal conversation appears to be automatic, we *can* train our minds to think what we want to think.

In general, if we think negatively, we feel worse about ourselves and others, have fewer positive ideas, and are more fatigued and less motivated to solve problems that may arise. Negative thoughts bring us down and are more likely to lead to poor results. On the other hand, positive thoughts make us feel good about ourselves and others, help us think of ways to solve problems we encounter, and give us more energy to solve problems. Positive thinking empowers us to do our best. Try this exercise:

1. For one day, pay attention to your thoughts and write some of them down.

2. Decide whether each of the thoughts was positive or negative.

3. Consider how each thought might have made you feel or act.

4. If a particular thought disempowered you, identify another thought that is useful or positive.

5. If you had a negative thought about a problem you are having, think of a positive way to solve it.

6. Take action! Do something to improve the situation you thought about.

7. Find a person who behaves and thinks in a way you admire and study that person as if you were completing an investigation or research project. Try to act and think the way they do.

---

or another and possibly in a combination of the four. A student may notice, for instance, that she is passive with adults at school, assertive with her friends, passive with the school bully, and passive-aggressive with her parents. Another student may notice that he is more likely to be assertive after earning a good score on a paper and that he tends to be aggressive after scoring poorly. Class discussions may be quite animated, interesting, and instructive for all. Because these definitions will be new to some, students may be surprised or concerned about their own behavior or that of people in their lives.

It is important to caution students about "practicing" assertive behavior with authority figures, because they may come across as aggressive when they don't intend to or may try to be assertive about inappropriate topics. It may be helpful to let parents and others know that students are learning how to be assertive, so that they have a context or

---

Figure 19.4

Definitions of Four Types of Behavior

Passive Behavior—Behavior that violates one's own rights. People who are passive don't express honest feelings and needs openly, or they express such needs in a self-effacing, self-degrading way that is apologetic and weak so that others may easily disregard them. The passive person often feels helpless and sees himself or herself as a victim. The message that the passive behavior sends is, "I am not important. What I think, feel, or need isn't important, so go ahead and take advantage of me." The position is "I lose/you win." Ultimately, both people lose ("lose/lose situation") because the other person never really knows who the passive person is, and the passive person often gives up and leaves the relationship.

Aggressive Behavior—Behavior that contains inappropriate expressions of emotions, usually anger, and violates the other person's rights. Aggressive behavior is usually aimed at dominating the other person, "winning" the situation, and forcing the other to lose. It is often humiliating and degrading to the other person and is designed to overpower the other, making him or her weaker and less able to defend his or her needs and rights. Its position is "I win/you lose." Over time, this is also a "lose/lose situation" because others distance themselves from the aggressive person, who is tolerated at best and usually disliked.

Passive-Aggressive Behavior—Behavior that is intended to express anger indirectly through such behaviors as being late, not finishing assignments or chores, or apologizing but not taking the action needed to follow through. Anger is hidden from the recipient and often from the passive-aggressive person as well. Passive-aggressive individuals are often bewildered by upset feelings that someone else might be experiencing, because they "didn't mean to do it" and seem confused about their level of responsibility. The passive-aggressive person gets the angry message across without taking responsibility for it. This position is "I win/you lose, but indirectly," again leading to a "lose/lose" relationship.

Assertive Behavior—Behavior that aims at maintaining self-respect while at the same time respecting the rights of others. It involves standing up for one's rights and needs and expressing oneself openly and honestly in appropriate ways that are not humiliating, dominating, or degrading to other people. The intended payoff is honest, effective communication between people so that a workable compromise can be reached that takes into account mutual respect and mutual concern for each other's rights, feelings, and needs. This is an "I win/you win" position, a "win/win" in the short run and the long run.

---

broader understanding for how students might be behaving.

One way to reinforce and build understanding about assertiveness is to introduce students to the Students' Bill of Assertive Rights presented in Figure 19.5, which builds on the work of Manuel Smith (1975), Robert Alberti (1983), and others. As an alternative, you might ask the class to develop a list of assertive rights. Either way, a class discussion

> **Figure 19.5**
> **Students' Bill of Assertive Rights**
>
> - I have the right to judge my own behavior and be responsible for it. I don't have the right to judge the behavior of others.
> - I have the right to not agree to help someone who isn't doing his or her own work.
> - I have the right to decide whether I need to find solutions to other people's problems, unless the other person is in danger. Then I have a duty to help someone who is in trouble, if I can, or to find an adult who can help.
> - I have the right to make mistakes and change my mind, but I need to make it right with whomever that affects.
> - I have the right not to like everyone. I don't have to be liked by everyone either, because there is no way that can happen anyway.
> - I have the right not to live in fear. I don't have the right to scare others.
> - I have the right to privacy and to not be gossiped about. I don't have the right to gossip.
> - I have the right to be treated with respect. I don't have the right to treat others disrespectfully.
> - I have the right to express my feelings in an assertive way.
> - I have the right to be taken seriously, and I need to take others seriously.
> - I have the right to say no without feeling bad. I don't have the right to force others into things they don't want to do.

can deepen students' understanding of what the statements contained in a bill of assertive rights mean in day-to-day life.

Being passive, aggressive, passive-aggressive, or assertive profoundly affects every area of a human being's life. No matter how we have behaved in the past, we can change our behavior if we are willing to look at it carefully and take steps to change it. Figure 19.6 provides a useful exercise to help students develop assertive behavior. The figure can be modified to incorporate opportunities for students to write. For example, you might ask students to use the details and ideas from the various exer-

cises to write a personal story or narrative about a fictitious character who succeeds in developing assertive behavior in his life.

Journal writing is another activity that can be used with many of the exercises described here to enhance students' understanding of assertive behavior. In many classes, students write in their journals and then turn them in to the teacher, who writes comments or thoughts before returning the journals to students. The teacher might ask specific students to comment on their assertive behavior (or lack thereof) and use the journal format as a way of engaging students in a discussion about their behavior.

Figure 19.6

How to Develop Assertive Behavior

Step 1. Keep a log of your behavior. Estimate the percentage of time in an average week that you are passive, aggressive, passive-aggressive, and assertive.

Step 2. Take a few minutes to think about your behavior more specifically. What exactly were you doing when you were passive, for example? What facial expressions and gestures were you using?

Step 3. List how your behavior affected your

- Self-esteem (feeling worthwhile, valuable, and capable)
- Achievement of goals
- Feelings (such as sadness, happiness, feeling down)
- Physical health
- Relationships with others

Step 4. See if you can spot any patterns in how you acted with certain people, at certain times of day, and in certain situations.

Step 5. Watch someone who is assertive—perhaps a friend or someone in the media—or think about an assertive character in a book or story. Study the person or character as if you were completing an investigation or a research project; notice the eye contact, facial expressions, and other aspects of the person or character whom you consider to be assertive.

Step 6. Mentally rehearse being assertive at all times. If you are thinking of the past, imagine being assertive if you were not. When you see yourself in the future, always see yourself being assertive. Mentally rehearsing passive, aggressive, or passive-aggressive behavior only reinforces that nonproductive behavior and makes those disappointing results more likely to happen.

Strategies for Conflict Prevention and Resolution

Along with helping students to reflect on the nature of responsibility and teaching students self-responsibility, the conflict resolution strategies discussed in this module help develop students' skills in self-management, self-respect, and self-reflection and self-observation, the foundation of a lifelong habit of personal responsibility. They also help students develop a sense of themselves as responsible and influential members of a community.

Recommendations for Classroom Practice

In this module, we discuss three specific ways to prevent and resolve conflict in the classroom:

- Developing a written statement of shared beliefs
- Using class meetings
- Teaching students specific strategies for conflict prevention and resolution

These strategies help build and deepen students' sense of responsibility for themselves and for their interactions with others, and ultimately their sense of self.

Developing a Written Statement of Shared Beliefs

Developing a written statement of shared beliefs lays the foundation for more effective conflict prevention and resolution. At least four

areas of responsibility may be appropriate to discuss with the class as a whole; they appear in the first half of Figure 20.1. These might be accompanied by brief statements of basic beliefs about how everyone will treat each other. You might first present the brief statements that appear in the figure in italics (e.g., "We are responsible for ourselves"); then, as a class, talk about what these mean and fill in examples. Or you might present everything shown in Figure 20.1 and ask students to react to the ideas and discuss what they mean using real-life examples.

Using Class Meetings

Class meetings—formal gatherings of students and teachers—can be a powerful tool for teaching and reinforcing behaviors that lead to enhanced self-management and responsibility. Among other benefits, effectively designed and led class meetings provide a structured, safe way for students to talk about issues; even students who do not speak during the meetings can benefit greatly. When one student speaks up in the classroom, he frequently voices thoughts, concerns, or feelings that other, less vocal students might have.

The value of effective class meetings lies in their development of students' abilities to

---

Figure 20.1

Shared Statements of Responsibility

For the Class as a Whole

1. *We are responsible for ourselves.* For example, we are responsible for our thoughts, feelings, behavior, physical health, possessions, and goals.

2. *We are responsible for how we treat others.* In particular, we are responsible for what we say and what we do to and with others.

3. *We have a part in how our peers and teachers treat us.* To a great extent, how others treat us is the result of how respectfully we interact with others, how assertive we are, and how clearly we've set our boundaries.

4. *We have a part in how well our environment works.* This means that we are part of how well the classroom functions, the extent to which materials and resources are kept in good condition, and how well we work together.

For Students as Individuals

1. I am responsible for me—for my feelings, my actions, my words, and my experience of my life.

2. Other people are responsible for themselves—for their feelings, actions, words, and experience of life.

3. I am 100-percent responsible for the consequences of my feelings, thoughts, actions, and words. Dealing with the consequences and rewards teaches me how to live in the world.

4. Other people are responsible for the consequences of their feelings, thoughts, actions, and words. Dealing with the consequences and rewards teaches them how to live in the world.

5. I am responsible for trying to make my school, my family, and the world a better place. If I see someone or something that is being harmed by another, it is my job to help or get an adult to help.

---

be effective participants in communities, large or small. As a microcosm of society as a whole, a classroom is touched by the same dynamics present in any group—differing opinions, thoughts, and points of view; the balance between the needs of individuals and the needs of the group; personal dynamics between individual students; and so on. Providing opportunities for students to discuss and resolve issues like these can result in fewer classroom problems and, thus, more

time for learning. Class meetings can also be effective ways of strengthening skills that will serve students in the long run, such as the following:

- Constructively voicing ideas and viewpoints
- Thinking creatively
- Problem solving with others
- Reflecting on one's own behaviors and their effect on others

- Responsibly communicating points of disagreement
- Respectfully discussing how others' behaviors affect you
- Respectfully and thoughtfully questioning others' ideas

Providing structured venues for class meetings can sow the seeds for students' future effective participation in their communities and in society as a whole. The simple act of setting aside time for students to talk together as a group communicates that the students' ideas and perspectives are valued.

You might set up regular class meetings or call a class meeting when a specific issue arises, being sure to model respectful listening and responsible communication and ensuring that those who wish to voice their ideas have opportunities to do so. Depending on students' age, maturity, and readiness, teachers should facilitate all class meetings initially but over time encourage and empower students to serve as facilitators.

Class meetings can take many forms. One teacher, for example, has identified a "peace table" in the classroom. The table has been set aside for talking over issues and outright conflicts, as well as "sore points" and areas of friction. Another teacher uses what she calls a "caring community" session. During the session, students discuss solutions to a specific problem and create a class plan of action. This allows students to reinforce each other in such areas as listening while others are speaking, praising others when appropriate, and speaking honestly but kindly and respectfully.

Regardless of the form of the class meeting, establishing specific strategies for the meeting

ensures that all voices are heard and that the discussion is not dominated by one or two students. For example, a high school teacher gives each student in the discussion two pennies. The idea is to allow each person his or her "two cents." When the person speaks, he or she puts two pennies in the middle of the table. That person is free to speak again, but only after everyone else in the group has spent their two cents.

One effective way to build student buy-in and responsibility and to reinforce basic principles for interacting during class meetings is to set and post a few simple but powerful guidelines, such as those listed in Figure 20.2.

Another effective tool that can be used in tandem with class meetings is a class meeting journal. Students might set aside a particular section of a notebook they already use for overall classroom items or use a special notebook just for this purpose. You might create a blank form with reflection questions, such as those listed in Figure 20.3. Although students might bring their journals to class meetings, a more useful approach is to reinforce the practice of students writing in their journals *after* the class meeting so that everyone is paying attention *during* the meeting.

Figure 20.2

Basic Principles for Class Meetings

We will be

- Respectful
- Honest and kind
- Careful listeners

Figure 20.3

Reflection Questions for a Class Meeting

1. In a sentence or two, how would you describe the issues discussed at the class meeting?

2. What was decided about the issue as a result of the meeting? How did the discussion end?

3. What thoughts, ideas, or reactions do you have about
   - The meeting and the discussion itself?
   - The decision that was made?
   - How the discussion ended?

4. In what ways do you think the meeting was useful or helpful?

5. Think about your participation in the class meeting. Even if you didn't speak or spoke very little, are you satisfied with your participation? If not, how can you use this experience to participate more effectively next time?

Teaching Students Specific Strategies for Conflict Prevention and Resolution

Human beings are different from one another. We have different backgrounds and personalities, different likes and dislikes, and different perspectives. As has often been said, "That's what makes the world go round." Between and among healthy, responsible individuals, our differences can make life richer and more rewarding. On the other hand, differences can lead to conflict and, unfortunately, at times to violence, as is readily apparent in any newspaper in any town.

One useful approach for helping students to prevent and resolve conflicts is to teach them active listening and speaking strategies, such as those discussed in Section 4, "Mental Set." Active listening and speaking is a structured way to have a conversation when the topic is difficult or when misunderstanding is likely to arise. Figure 20.4 includes an abbreviated version of the exercise for teachers described in more detail in Figure 17.1 in Section 4.

An important issue related to conflict resolution and prevention is the topic of emotions. Although teachers are not psychologists, they (and other appropriate school personnel, such as counselors) can help students learn to deal with their emotions, particularly feelings of anger. People of all ages have difficulty appropriately dealing with their feelings, particularly when it comes to anger. Such feelings can seem to come out of nowhere; at times, they can feel uncontrollable. Anger can damage relationships, health, and feelings of self-worth. Unchecked anger frequently leads to violence. Although it

---

Figure 20.4
Active Listening and Speaking for Students

The essence of this exercise is that students practice listening carefully while someone else is speaking and develop their skill in being able to restate exactly what someone else said—nothing more, nothing less.

1. Ask each pair of students to decide who will be the first speaker for the exercise and who will be the listener.

2. The student who is the first speaker should say a few things about his or her perspectives or feelings about a particular topic. (This can be a real topic that is causing conflict or disagreement or an imaginary topic.) Explain, and model, that speakers should try to use only "I" statements describing themselves only—for instance, "I feel hurt about what happened today at lunch" rather than, "I think you were a jerk today."

3. The student who is the first listener should say back to the speaker what the listener heard the speaker say—for example, "What I heard you say is that you are feeling hurt about what happened at lunch." The listener should not express any of his or her own opinions or reactions to what the speaker said, even if the listener is *thinking* these things!

4. The student who was the speaker should say whether the listener has accurately restated the speaker's perspective. If not, the speaker should calmly restate what he or she said until the listener is able to paraphrase it accurately, including the feelings of the speaker.

5. This may be repeated two or three times.

6. Now the students switch roles—the listener becomes the speaker and the speaker becomes the listener. Monitor the time to ensure that students have an equal opportunity to express themselves and be heard.

---

may be difficult to do, anger can and should be controlled.

Anger is a biologically wired emotion, part of nature's fight-or-flight mechanism that ensures the survival of the human species. It is the most misunderstood and misused emotion, one that has created the most havoc in the history of the world and in individual lives. It need

not remain mysterious, but rather can be understood and used well.

Figure 20.5 includes a strategy that teachers and guidance counselors might share with students for dealing with angry feelings toward others. In addition, students should be encouraged to talk with their parents about any particularly upsetting thoughts or feelings they are having.

Figure 20.5

Dealing with Anger

1. Recognize when you are first becoming angry.

   a. Look for negative thoughts such as "I hate you" or "Shut up."

   b. Notice body reactions such as shallow breathing, tight jaw, and clenched fists.

   c. See if you are just trying to win the argument or make the other person wrong (a win/lose situation), rather than trying to solve the problem in a way that works for both of you (a win/win situation).

2. Take a time-out.

   a. Tell the other person you are taking a time-out to cool down. If you continue to argue, the conversation will only get worse and more destructive.

   b. Take a few deep breaths or take a walk to help your body calm down. Don't punch pillows or punching bags; dramatizing your anger in this way doesn't lessen your anger.

   c. Write down negative thoughts you are having about yourself and the other person.

   d. Now write down what is positive about yourself and the other person.

   e. Think about how what you did or said contributed to the conflict. See if you can be responsible for what you did or said, or what you *didn't* say or do that you think you should have.

3. Return to the situation.

   a. Tell the other person one thing that is positive about him or her.

   b. Tell the other person what you did to make the conversation become negative.

   c. Let the other person tell you what he or she did to make the conversation not work. If the other person is not able or willing to do so, don't use this as an excuse to get angry again. The other person may need more time to think about what happened.

   d. When both of you have calmed down, try to restart the conversation and do your part to have it stay on track. Look for a solution that works for both of you. If you find that you are getting angry again, or the conversation is getting overly heated, take another time-out.

■ Section Reflection

Checking Your Understanding

Use the space provided to write your answers to the questions.

- Two students, Amy and Jacquie, are involved in an argument. Both of them independently come to see you. They are angry and blaming the other person for what happened. What should you do or say?

- A student named June asks to see you after class; she is clearly upset. She says she has been harassed by another student who says her name is "dumb," and now she's wondering whether she's "responsible," given the discussion in class. What should you do or say? And how might you use the ideas about assertiveness to help June in this situation?

- Fiona and Robert worked on a project together. Now Fiona is taking all of the credit for the project, but you know that Robert did more than his share of the work. What should you do? What might you say to Fiona? To Robert?

- Jesse has repeatedly not turned in his homework on time. You made it clear that part of the grade at the end of the semester would reflect the student's timeliness in turning in assignments. How might you use the principles of personal responsibility to support Jesse *before* the end of the semester?

- David is a very vocal student. Every week since the beginning of the semester he has proposed a class meeting. Often his reasons have been sound and the goals of the meeting have been on target. But increasingly it seems as though David is using the meetings just to complain and to get other students to agree with him. What should you do?

- The class meeting you held last week was a disaster! It started out with a specific topic as the focal point, and a constructive conversation was taking place. But suddenly it deteriorated and several students left upset. Now no one wants to talk about what happened—or anything else for that matter. What should you do?

A Self-Assessment

Circle the number on the scale that best matches your situation, with 0 indicating "Not at all" and 4 indicating "To a great extent."

I incorporate ideas about personal responsibility into my instruction and classroom practice.

I make sure that students understand when it is appropriate to take responsibility for their actions and when it is not.

I help students learn to develop assertive behavior, rather than passive, passive-aggressive, or aggressive behavior.

I reinforce the value of positive self-talk with my students.

I use class meetings and other strategies to prevent and resolve classroom conflicts.

6

GETTING OFF TO A GOOD START

In this section, we deal with techniques and considerations that teachers can use to begin the year well. Effective classroom teachers begin instituting their management regimen on the first day of class. In fact, managing behavior with the goal of effective learning must start *before* the first day of school.

The different things teachers can and should do to set the right tone for classroom management range from the concrete to the subtle—from arranging the chairs, desks, and other physical objects in the room to establishing a foundation for effective relationships with students. This section is divided into three modules that address the planning for management that should occur before school begins and the actions that should occur at the very beginning of the school year to allow both the students and the teacher to get off to a good start:

- Module 21: Before School Begins
- Module 22: The First Day of School
- Module 23: The First Two Weeks of School

■ Reflecting on Your Current Beliefs and Practices

Before reading the modules in this section, take some time to reflect on your beliefs, perspectives, and current practices with regard to getting off to a good start. Then write your answers to the following questions in the space provided. Your responses will give you a basis for comparison as you read about the strategies recommended in these modules.

- What are some of the things you think about when organizing your classroom at the beginning of the year?

- What do you do during the first few weeks of school to build strong relationships with students?

- What activities will you use to help students get to know you and each other?

- What are some of the rules and procedures that must be taught in the first days of school? How will you involve students in generating these?

- List three to five rules you set that help ensure an atmosphere of comfort, safety, and order.

- What activities do you use to practice routines and procedures?

- What feedback systems do you have in place to reinforce students for following routines and procedures during the first few weeks of school?

Before School Begins

Effective classroom management begins even *before* students arrive at school. Most students who walk into class on the first day are hardly aware of the time, attention, and effort that responsible teachers have put into every aspect of the teaching and learning environment.

Recommendations for Classroom Practice

This module highlights three broad strategies to lay a strong foundation for good classroom management before school begins:

- Organizing and preparing the physical space
- Laying the foundation for strong teacher-student relationships
- Preparing rules, procedures, and academic expectations

Organizing and Preparing the Physical Space

The physical surroundings in which we work, study, and play can greatly influence our satisfaction and sense of focus and effectiveness. The same can be said for the physical space of the classroom. How the classroom is organized and decorated can either contribute to or detract from creating a good environment for teaching and learning for students and teachers alike. Regardless of how the classroom is arranged, an atmosphere of comfort, safety,

and order is a critical backdrop for effective learning.

The overriding principle for classroom organization is to create a set of physical conditions that are an advantage to you as a teacher. Studies show that one of the most effective deterrents to off-task behavior is teacher proximity. Desk arrangements should provide the teacher with access to any student in the room in three or four steps from where the teacher spends most of the instructional time. The arrangements should also provide for easy access to and storage of materials, as well as clear traffic pathways. Figures 21.1 and 21.2 present possible room arrangements for elementary and secondary classrooms, respectively.

Using these configurations, many teachers, particularly elementary teachers, assign seats for students. Assigned seating lets students know that they have a space in the room and a "territory" of their own. It provides an immediate sense of belonging for students and lessens their anxiety as they enter the room every day. In the alternative, teachers allow students to select their own seats on the first day of school. One advantage of this approach is that it gives students some responsibility for the learning environment.

At the elementary level, we suggest that teachers put nameplates on students' desks and give students an opportunity to decorate their

Figure 21.1

Possible Arrangement of an Elementary Classroom

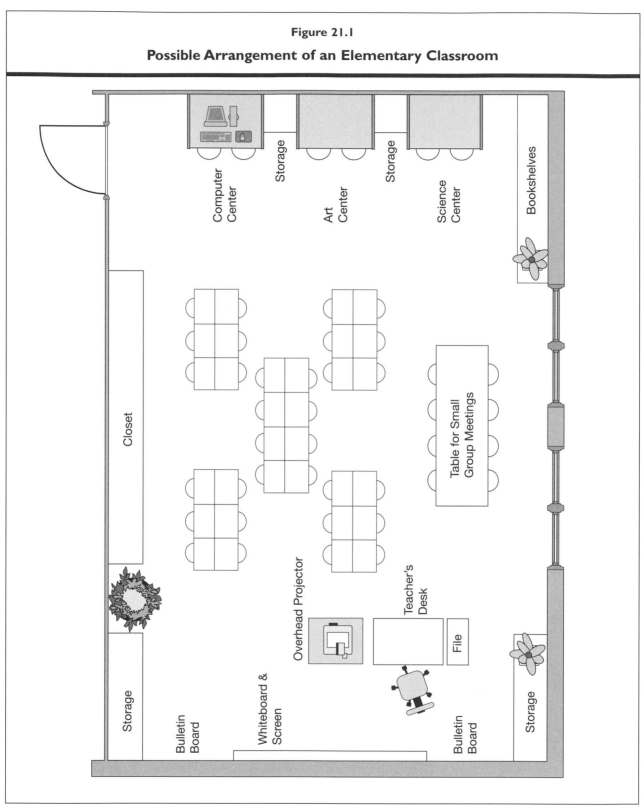

Source: Marzano, R. J. (with Marzano, J. S., & Pickering, D. J.). (2003). *Classroom Management That Works.* Alexandria, VA: Association for Supervision and Curriculum Development, p. 95. Copyright 2003 by ASCD. Reprinted by permission.

Figure 21.2

Possible Arrangement of a Secondary Classroom

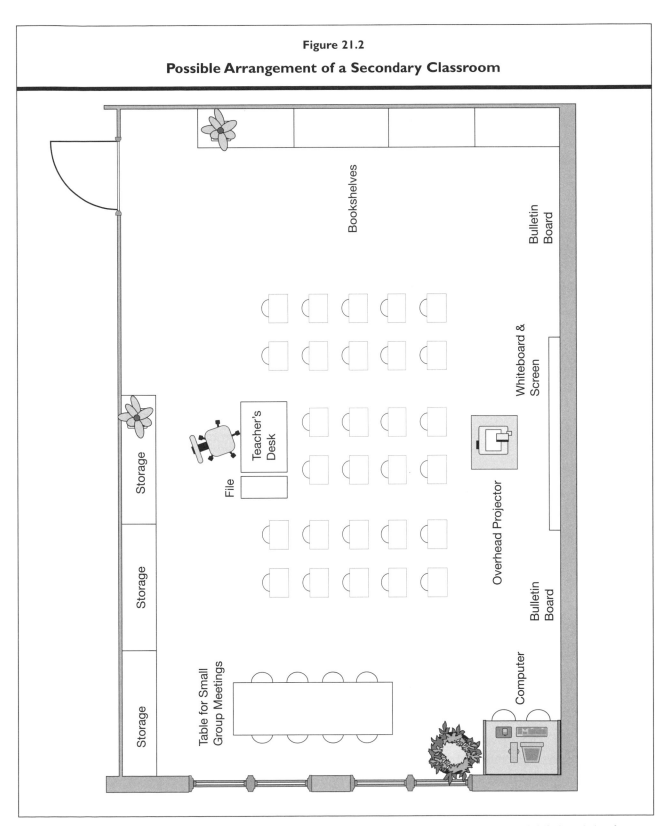

Source: Marzano, R. J. (with Marzano, J. S., & Pickering, D. J.). (2003). *Classroom Management That Works.* Alexandria, VA: Association for Supervision and Curriculum Development, p. 97. Copyright 2003 by ASCD. Reprinted by permission.

nameplates periodically during the year. At the secondary level, we suggest that teachers use assigned seats as a "home base" for alternate seating arrangements during the year. Either way, a desk and seating organization that allows for student interaction sets the stage for successful icebreaker activities that can help form positive teacher-student relationships as well as relationships among students.

Classroom Management That Works (Marzano, 2003, pp. 94–98) presents a number of guidelines for arranging classrooms. As you arrange and decorate your classroom, you might also consider the issues presented in Figure 21.3.

Laying the Foundation for Strong Teacher-Student Relationships

As we discussed in Section 3, the relationships that you develop with your students are a significant factor in a well-organized and well-managed classroom. If the relationships are good, you have laid an important foundation for a satisfying and effective learning environment. You can and should do a number of things even before the start of the school year to lay the groundwork for good relationships with students and set the right tone for the classroom. Here are some examples:

• Send each student (and possibly parents as well) a short personalized note.
• Call each student and welcome him or her to the class.
• Talk with students' previous teachers.
• Learn about students' interests and activities by reading the school newspaper and talking with teachers of special classes.
• Create a "getting-to-know-you" activity for the first few days of school (see the next

module for further description). Prepare any materials that might be needed for this activity.

One teacher, for example, sends postcards to each student on her class list to introduce herself. On the card, she tells students how excited she is to have them in her class and describes what a wonderful year they will have together. She also mentions some of the activities they will be doing during the year and includes a return address.

A key aspect of successful teacher-student relationships is successful teacher-parent relationships. As we describe in Section 2, "Discipline and Consequences," if you take the time to meet with parents, develop a rapport with them, and familiarize them with behavioral expectations and disciplinary consequences, you are more likely to have good results when you need to call parents later in the year about problems. Actions you might take include scheduling an orientation luncheon, mailing an orientation packet to parents, or calling and meeting with parents.

Preparing Rules, Procedures, and Academic Expectations

As the first day of school approaches, you can do several things to make sure that the classroom is ready for students—and that you are, too!—and to communicate the idea that the classroom is a place for structured learning:

• Make sure that the initial learning goals for the first few weeks of class are clearly stated on the board or overhead image. Develop a course syllabus that lists major deadline dates.
• Have a sponge activity (a warm-up activity or day-starter) ready on the board or on an overhead image for students to begin the day.

Figure 21.3

Things to Consider in Arranging a Classroom

Students' Desks and Chairs and the Teacher's Work Area

- How many students will be in the class?
- Does the room's layout present any safety issues?
- Where will whole-group instruction take place?
- Will all students be able to easily see you during whole-group instruction or see other students who are making presentations?
- Where is the storage area for materials you will use most frequently for whole-group instruction?
- Where is the blackboard or whiteboard located?
- If you will use an overhead projector, what is the best placement for that?
- To what extent will you be pairing students or creating small groups for learning?
- What seating arrangement will best encourage student discussion and productive interaction?
- Should you place your desk at the front of the room or the back of the room?
- Regardless of where you place your desk, can you easily see all students and make eye contact with them as needed?

Access to Learning Centers, Technology, and Equipment

- How many centers are needed?
- What are the primary patterns of movement around the class?
- Should some centers be close to particular books, materials, or other resources?
- What is the best placement for computers and printers?
- Do certain materials and equipment require special placement for safety reasons (for example, chemicals, lab equipment)?
- Where might bookshelves be easily accessed, but not create traffic jams?

Decorating the Room

- Where is the door to the classroom—what do you want students to see as they enter and leave the room?
- Are wall spaces available for bulletin boards, calendars, and displays to post learning goals, assignments, special announcements, and student work? What is the best placement for these things?
- Will you be creating a poster with pockets for each student?
- How much empty space should you leave for later use?
- What else might need to be displayed—for example, the alphabet, poems, vocabulary lists, classroom rules, the daily timeline, standards or learning goals?

(continued)

Figure 21.3

Things to Consider in Arranging a Classroom *(continued)*

Materials

It is extremely helpful to have most of the necessary materials ready before students arrive on the first day of school. Depending on students' grade level, the content area, and the types of lessons and units you have planned, you might want to have the following materials prepared and organized:

- Pens, pencils, and paper
- Paper clips, staplers, and staples
- Music and a CD player
- Band-Aids, tissues, and any other first-aid equipment your school requires
- Attendance materials, class sheets, and seating charts
- In/out boxes for collected papers and transparencies
- An extra bulb for the overhead projector
- Sticky notes and name tags

In addition, think about

- What materials will be needed for the lessons and units planned for the first few weeks of school?
- What materials and resources may need to be ordered now for later use?

Plan how to establish an appropriate, professional atmosphere for learning from the time students enter the class to the time you dismiss the class.

• Plan for and schedule class meeting times to give feedback on how students are doing in following established class rules and procedures.

• Prepare and practice your welcoming remarks for students. You should strive for a good balance between warmth and structure. In particular, you should convey the sense that you are available to students and supportive of them as individuals and as a class, while making it clear that rules and structures are in place to ensure that the classroom learning environment is well managed, safe, comfortable for everyone, and orderly.

• Write down and rehearse the lesson plan for the first day. You'll get only one chance to make an effective impression, and the first day is a poor time to "wing it."

The First Day of School

We deal with the first day of school as a separate module because it is probably the most important day of the school year in establishing a well-managed classroom. It is the linchpin for effective classroom management for teachers, and thus the crux of effective learning for students.

Recommendations for Classroom Practice

This module focuses on the following aspects of the first day of school:

- Familiarizing students with the classroom and seating arrangements
- Using icebreaker exercises and other getting-to-know-you activities
- Establishing rules, expectations, and academics as the framework for the classroom

Familiarizing Students with the Classroom and Seating Arrangements

Even if some students are not new to your class, on the first day of school it is a good idea to take a few minutes to conduct a "room tour" after students take their seats. This orientation can help students become familiar with the unique aspects of the room, such as where learning centers are located, where student work will be displayed, where resource materials are kept, and where there might be safety considerations (related to such things as laboratory chemicals or specialty equipment, for example).

In terms of seating arrangements, let students know where they will be sitting and direct them to the seat with their nameplate, or provide time for them to choose a seat where they feel comfortable. If you take the latter approach, explain to students at the beginning of class that the choice is theirs as long as the seat they choose is optimal for learning for them and the students sitting around them. You might give students the option of changing their seat on Day 2; in most cases, however, students will sit in the same spot they chose on the first day.

Using Icebreaker Exercises and Other Getting-to-Know-You Activities

An important step during the first day of class is introducing yourself to students, welcoming them to the class, and helping them to begin the process of getting to know one another as well. There are many ways to do this, both informal and formal.

A Classroom Door Meet-and-Greet. Stand at the door, greet students, and introduce yourself—saying, for example, "Hi, I'm Mrs. Greenfield. Welcome to English 9."

A Seat-Based Welcome. As students work on the sponge activity for the day, circulate around the room. Welcome each student quietly and personally, and, if you have given students the option to select their seats, write the student's name phonetically on a seating chart. (This also is an easy way to take attendance.)

A Front-of-the Room Introduction. Wait until all students have arrived and taken a seat, and then introduce yourself. In addition to your name, you might mention the name of the class, how many years you have taught at the school or in the subject area, and perhaps something about the subject, school, or class that you are particularly excited about or interested in. Refer to any welcoming remarks you prepared before school began.

A Nametag Getting-to-Know-You Activity. Design a nametag for yourself with the title of one of your favorite books. Explain why the book is one of your favorites and why you recommend it to others. You might have students design similar nametags for themselves, identifying their favorite book on the nametag. Students and teacher might then stand, move around the room, and introduce themselves to at least five others. You can model this by saying, "Hi, I'm Mrs. Greenfield. A favorite read of mine is *The Secret Life of Bees*. Here's why I would recommend the book to you. . . ."

"Icebreaker" Activities. You can use a variety of ways to "break the ice" between yourself and students and among students:

• Simply ask students to introduce themselves by name.

• Provide time for brief introductions, and then ask students to take a couple of minutes to introduce themselves to someone they didn't know before they walked into class.

• Decorate students' desks with personalized nameplates and include a set of pencils or crayons, paper, and a notebook. The first page of the notebook should be titled "Tell Me About Yourself" and include some focus questions around personal interests. Arrange the desks in groups of four so students can share their interests.

• Use a "placemat" activity to help students get to know each other. Group students in teams of four and have each student sit at a corner of a large square of poster-size paper. Ask students to list a little information about themselves in each corner (for example, family members, favorite music, sports heroes, favorite video or movie). Then have them share this information and list the items they have in common in a square in the center of the paper. The students decide on a team name for themselves and share the poster and the team name with their classmates. Posters are then displayed around the classroom.

• Engage students in other get-acquainted games, such as the one outlined in Figure 22.1.

Establishing Rules, Expectations, and Academics as the Framework for the Classroom

Depending on students' grade level, you might use or adapt the following sequence to teach, discuss, and begin to reinforce classroom rules and expectations for behavior:

1. Begin a discussion of rules and expectations by modeling and teaching a cue for getting students' attention. The cue might come in handy as soon as class begins! For example, use the raised-hand cue as a gesture for bringing the class to silence and focus without raising your

Figure 22.1

Getting Acquainted Activity: "True" or "False"

Time: One session, 15 minutes

Materials: Paper and pencils

Procedure:

1. Divide students into groups of four.

2. Each student writes two statements about himself or herself that are true and one statement that is false.

3. In turn, each student reads his or her list and the group members try to decide which statement is false.

4. Ask for a few volunteers who are willing to read their statements in front of the whole class and have the class respond.

voice. The idea is to keep your voice calm and quiet and to avoid raising your voice to get students' attention. Simply raise your hand to signal that it's time to focus on you, the teacher; students then raise their hands and direct their attention to you or whomever is speaking.

2. Set the stage for telling students how important rules and procedures are by asking them what would happen if there were no rules about how people should treat one another, drive cars, or respect their own and others' property.

3. Discuss appropriate ways students can remind one another to focus attention on the teacher or whomever is speaking to the class.

4. If you are involving students in the process of establishing rules and appropriate consequences or giving them a chance to offer their input on these, begin this process now.

5. If you have already established rules and consequences for the class, explain the need for the most important rules for your classroom (for example, you might explain one rule for interpersonal relationships, one rule for academics, and the top rule for safety).

6. Ask students to give examples of what these rules look like in practice at school. A good lead-in is a discussion about the kinds of rules students must follow at home or in society.

7. Show students the sequence of nonverbal teacher reactions you will use when you notice that someone has broken a rule or is about to break a rule.

8. Go over the consequences for breaking rules.

9. Depending on students' age, you may want to practice the most important classroom rules every day until students have mastered them.

10. With younger students in particular, practice the daily procedure for entering the room, sitting in seats, and beginning work on the sponge activity. For example, have fun role-playing examples—and nonexamples—of appropriate ways to enter the room and begin working on the day-starter. Students need a clear picture of what you mean when you ask them to set a focused, respectful atmosphere for learning.

11. Periodically review and practice the rules at longer-spaced intervals. Keep practicing until *all* students can perform the rules and procedures correctly.

Learning academic content in different subject areas is obviously one of the primary purposes of schooling. On the first day of school, this attention on learning content-area knowledge and skills should be made very clear. You can do this in a number of ways:

• Make sure the learning goal or goals are clearly stated on the board or on an overhead image. Explain that the learning goal will be communicated every day.

• Direct students to the sponge activity (warm-up, day-starter), which should be displayed on the board or on an overhead image for students to start the day.

• Discuss your philosophy of teaching and learning and your commitment to students.

• Ask students to describe their own philosophy of learning and commitment to the learning environment.

• Explain what students will be learning; distribute a syllabus of learning goals for the year.

• Explain to students that the daily routine will include a sponge activity, discussion of the daily learning goal or goals, review and follow-up of the previous day's work and homework, teacher-led instruction or explanation of student-centered work, closure, and explanation of the homework assignment.

The First Two Weeks of School

In this module, we deal with strategies and techniques that you can use to get off to a good start during the first two weeks of school. We deal with the first two weeks of school as a separate module because these weeks set the stage for the rest of the year.

Recommendations for Classroom Practice

The first two weeks of school is a time when students and teachers build relationships, set expectations for learning, and reinforce the routines for classroom management and curriculum implementation. This module focuses on the following aspects of the first two weeks of school:

- Building relationships
- Setting and reinforcing academic and nonacademic expectations and routines

Building Relationships

Building relationships with and among students is a process that goes on throughout the school year. But during the first two weeks of school, you can do a number of specific things to build on the foundation you laid before school began and on the first day of school. The attention you pay to this critical area will pay

off in the long run. Specific actions you can take include the following:

- Learn the names of students—including correct pronunciation—as soon as possible.
- Survey students to learn about their personal interests and hobbies (see Section 3, Module 12, "Demonstrating Personal Interest in Students").
- Organize a "Person of the Week" bulletin board where students display photos, ribbons, medals, and other artifacts that represent who they are and what they are interested in outside of school.
- Display your own family pictures, artifacts, awards, and high school and college diplomas on the wall so students have an opportunity to get to know you more personally.
- Create a "You Are a Star" display in the classroom. Each student decorates a star with his or her name and adds five personal bits of information—one on each point of the star. Hang the star on string from the ceiling in the classroom so each student is represented as a "star" personality. Have sticky notes available for students to write compliments to one another and attach to the stars hanging from the ceiling. Encourage students to compliment one another on academic and nonacademic performance

that demonstrates "star" quality. For example, comments can be written recognizing academic improvement and progress, staying on task, participation, effort on assignments, or cooperation with others. Model the activity several times so students become familiar with what you mean by "star quality" comments.

• Call all parents during the first two weeks of school and let them know how pleased you are to have their children in your classroom. Continue to call parents throughout the year about the positive things that you see in their children.

• Invite parents to join your class at any time and participate in the learning with their children.

• Involve students in decisions about policies that affect their comfort, safety, and order in the classroom, such as taking bathroom breaks, getting a drink of water, going to their locker for materials, and treating others with respect.

Setting and Reinforcing Academic and Nonacademic Expectations and Routines

As we have noted several times throughout this book, setting routines is only part of ensuring that a classroom is well managed. These expectations must be reinforced and maintained throughout the school year. The first two weeks are an especially critical time for cementing behavioral expectations for academic routines and processes. Toward this end, you might implement the following strategies:

• Clarify and communicate the learning goals for each class period or lesson.

• Clarify and communicate the behavioral goals for each class period or lesson.

• Know the essential knowledge that all students should learn from the standards or learning goals. Communicate the essential knowledge to students within the first two weeks of school.

• Administer a pretest to students to determine levels of proficiency within the class. Plan for flexible groups to meet the needs of various learners.

• Develop lesson plans for the first two weeks before the weeks actually begin. Two weeks' worth of lesson plans will guide you and allow for revisions based on students' needs.

• Develop rubrics with students for various learning goals and nonacademic goals. Seek students' input when developing criteria for levels of performance.

• Make sure students are clear about relevant district, state, and school-level standards and benchmarks.

• Provide students with a homework policy. (See, for example, Marzano, Pickering, & Pollock, 2001, p. 121.)

• Provide students with a clear grading policy.

• Provide students with a course guide or syllabus for the semester or the year.

• Establish a routine for the class period or school day. For example, begin each class with a sponge activity. During class time, discuss learning goals and behavior expectations, present an overview of the agenda, involve students in the learning activity or activities, and include a closing activity at the end of the lesson.

• Establish expectations for ongoing assignments such as those that might be part of an English or science notebook, or expectations for an ongoing journal-writing assignment.

• Practice providing timely feedback to students. (See Marzano, Norford, Paynter, Pickering, & Gaddy, 2001, pp. 185–196.)

• Monitor students' learning. (See Marzano et al., 2001, pp. 97–115, for suggestions on reinforcing effort and providing recognition.)

• Set up and communicate a schedule for the class or the day, such as that shown in Figure 23.1. Schedules can help students stay on track and build their responsibility for time management.

• Practice routines for handing in homework; leaving the classroom; entering the classroom; transitioning between activities; moving around the room; handing in materials; and working in pairs, small groups, and large groups. Take time to practice and give feedback to students on their performance.

Figure 23.1 **Sample Class Schedule**	
8:30	Morning work
8:50	Writing
9:30	Language arts
10:20	Reading
11:05	Lunch
11:45	Study time
12:05	Math
1:25	Social studies
2:15	Pack up/planner time
2:30	Review homework/answer questions

• Discuss rubrics for participation, effort, achievement, and homework.

• Role-play appropriate and inappropriate behaviors for routines and procedures. Have fun with the class as you establish the point.

■ Section Reflection

Checking Your Understanding
Use the space provided to write your answers to the questions.

• It's your first year at this school, and you walk into your classroom for the first time. You begin to think about how to organize students' seats and desks, your desk, books and other resources, learning centers, and so on. What should be your highest priorities?

• Most of the students in your class already know each other, but there are a few new students. You have a couple of "getting-to-know-you" exercises that you have used in the past. How might you vary these given the makeup of your current class?

• At a staff retreat, the topic of student buy-in arises. Someone says that students should always be allowed to select their own seats when they arrive in class. Do you agree with this? Why or why not?

- You have taught elementary students for many years. But this summer you accepted a position at a middle school. As you plan for the upcoming year, what will you do differently? What will your focus be?

- The first day of school went well. But now that a few days have gone by, your relationships with some students seem rocky, even though you sent letters to each student before school started and have made an effort to use students' names each time you interact with them. What are some of the strategies you might use to strengthen your relationships with students over the next couple of weeks?

- You spent time planning your lessons for the first couple of weeks of school. But students seem confused about what, specifically, they are supposed to be learning. What might you do to clarify this and to reinforce the connection between standards and specific lessons?

A Self-Assessment

Circle the number on the scale that best matches your situation, with 0 indicating "Not at all" and 4 indicating "To a great extent."

I have arranged my classroom to reflect comfort, safety, and order.

I have arranged my classroom so that students can see all presentations, find needed materials, and group themselves in a variety of ways.

I have identified and established a set of routines, rules, and procedures.

I have planned how to communicate classroom expectations to students.

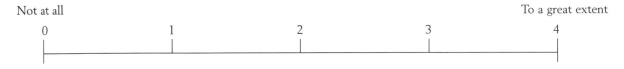

I have planned activities for the first day that will engage students and help them get to know each other and me.

I have developed my lesson plans and specific learning goals for at least the first few weeks of class.

I have developed clear policies for homework and grading and clear ways in which to help students understand these.

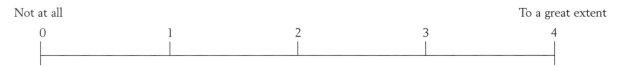

I have determined how I will communicate with parents about this new school year and my classroom expectations.

7

Management at the School Level

Thus far we have considered management at the classroom level—specifically, those practices and behaviors that a classroom teacher must implement and the responsibilities that individual students learn to assume to ensure that the classroom is a well-managed, healthy environment for learning. In this set of modules, we address school-level management. As Marzano (2003) notes in *Classroom Management That Works*, "school-level management and classroom-level management have a symbiotic relationship" (p. 103). This relationship is symbiotic because from the student perspective, an effectively managed school includes both interactions with individual teachers and a sense of safety and order in common areas, such as hallways, the playground, the cafeteria, or the parking lot, and while participating in assemblies and other all-school activities.

School-level management provides the broader context in which classroom management occurs. If management at the school level is disorganized or lax, management at the classroom level will be negatively influenced. If school-level management is systematic and crisp, it is more likely that classroom management will follow suit.

This section is made of up two modules that address key areas of school-level management:

• Module 24: Establishing and Enforcing Schoolwide Rules, Procedures, and Consequences
• Module 25: Establishing Norms of Conduct for Faculty and Staff

■ Reflecting on Your Current Beliefs and Practices

Before reading the modules in this section, take some time to reflect on your beliefs, your perspectives, and the current school-level management practices in your school. Then answer the following questions in the space provided. Your responses will give you a basis for comparison as you read about the strategies recommended in these modules.

• Why is it a good idea to establish schoolwide rules, procedures, and consequences?

• Who should be involved in setting these schoolwide expectations for behavior?

• What are some of the specific rules, procedures, and consequences that might be appropriate for the elementary and secondary levels?

• What are some ways in which your school communicates schoolwide rules and procedures to students, parents, and other stakeholders?

• Describe how your school uses a discipline hierarchy and how it is enforced.

• Has your school established a safety and discipline committee or team? If so, what kinds of specific issues has the team addressed?

• Describe some norms of conduct that your staff has agreed to manage on their own.

Establishing and Enforcing Schoolwide Rules, Procedures, and Consequences

One way that a school communicates a strong sense of order—or lack thereof—is through the schoolwide rules and procedures it initiates and the consequences it establishes for violations of those rules and procedures. Schoolwide rules, procedures, and consequences are set for general areas ranging from bullying or verbal harassment to theft, gang behavior, and use of drugs.

Although students often chafe at the idea of rules and consequences, experienced teachers and school leaders know that clear, specific rules and consequences create a sense of order and safety for all students. In fact, students appreciate structure, though they may not speak or act as if they do!

Recommendations for Organizational Practice

In this module, we consider five actions that school leaders should take to establish and enforce schoolwide rules, procedures, and consequences:

- Establishing a safety and discipline committee
- Creating a discipline hierarchy
- Establishing procedures and practices for potentially hazardous events and locations
- Communicating expectations to students and others
- Developing a system to track behavioral issues in the school

Establishing a Safety and Discipline Committee

One of the first orders of business in school-level management is to establish a safety and discipline committee. This committee is a group of individuals who voluntarily assume responsibility for the management of the entire school, not just their individual classrooms. In effect, the safety and discipline committee is responsible for establishing and maintaining the management activities in every aspect of the school other than the management of individual classrooms. Putting together an effective safety and discipline committee involves enlisting a representative group of teachers by grade level and discipline (regular education, special education, electives, and teaching assistants). The committee should also have a parent representative, and, at higher grade levels, a student representative. Given the critical importance of safety and discipline to the overall school, this committee should be overseen by the principal or the assistant principal.

The overall function of the safety and discipline committee is to act as a data-gathering body that makes recommendations, supplies information, and develops policies and procedures for schoolwide safety and order. In addition to establishing schoolwide safety rules, procedures, and consequences, the safety and discipline committee carries out a range of specific responsibilities, including the following:

- Designating interior locations for "duck and cover" tornado drills
- Assisting with these drills at least twice a year
- Monitoring exit times during monthly fire evacuation drills
- Debriefing staff on the efficiency of evacuation procedures
- Coordinating the supervision and security for evening schoolwide events (for example, carnivals, music events, dances)
- Monitoring and communicating concerns about student attendance to parents and preparing reports to school administrators for follow-up if necessary

Another responsibility of the committee is to prepare presentations about safety and discipline for parents during orientation or back-to-school night. Parents who understand the school's policies and procedures are partners in creating and maintaining a safe, well-managed, and effective school environment.

Since the September 11, 2001, attacks on the United States, safety and discipline committees in most schools have expanded the scope of their safety procedures to include preparation and training regarding biohazard, chemical, and physical dangers and lockdown procedures.

These drills should be practiced at least twice a year, and staff members should be regularly briefed on compliance.

Creating a Discipline Hierarchy

At the school level, one of the most powerful steps that can be taken is to institute a discipline hierarchy. In simple terms, a discipline hierarchy identifies categories or levels of behavioral issues and the manner in which those issues will be addressed. Some issues are addressed by classroom teachers; others are handled outside of the classroom. Such a system sends a strong message to students, parents, and guardians—namely, that the rules, procedures, and disciplinary consequences within individual classrooms and across the school are well coordinated and consistent. The student views management not as an individual issue from teacher to teacher but as a unified whole.

A discipline hierarchy also helps individual classroom teachers—who may or may not be highly skilled in management techniques—because it provides them with visible backing. With the design of a discipline hierarchy, students (and parents) become aware that certain types of misbehavior will automatically be dealt with at a "higher level" than the individual classroom teacher. A discipline hierarchy communicates to students and parents that being in the classroom is a privilege and that certain minimum behaviors are required to earn the right to that privilege.

The action required to establish a discipline hierarchy is straightforward: identify levels of misbehavior and determine how each level will be addressed. In this module, we consider three levels:

- *Level 1* behavioral offenses are those that are to be addressed in the classroom.
- *Level 2* behavioral offenses are those that are to be addressed by school administrators or the safety and discipline committee.
- *Level 3* behavioral offenses are those that warrant immediate suspension or expulsion.

These levels are examples only. That is, depending on the grade levels served by a school, administrators might decide to establish more levels than the three described here.

Level 1 Offenses. These offenses are to be handled by the classroom teacher. Recall from Section 1 that each classroom teacher will establish a few rules and procedures at the beginning of the year (for example, "Do not disturb others who are working," "Respect school and personal property," "Follow directions"). By definition, Level 1 offenses occur when students violate the rules and procedures that have been established by individual classroom teachers. Such violations lead to consequences that may involve the following:

- Verbal warning
- Time-out
- A meeting with parents
- A visit to the principal's office
- A written or verbal apology from the student

Each grade-level team should submit a Level 1 discipline plan to the principal, keep its own record of infractions and consequences by student, and document communication with parents regarding student behavior. Teams should meet monthly with the principal to review data related to Level 1 discipline situations.

Level 2 Offenses. These offenses are addressed outside of the classroom by school administrators (such as the principal or assistant principal), by the safety and discipline committee, or by both. Level 2 behavioral offenses are above and beyond violations of classroom rules and procedures and are typically viewed as "serious misconduct" offenses. They are behaviors that are causing a major disruption in the classroom, and they are chronic and continuous. Typically, these offenses include the following types of behavior:

- Fighting
- Repeated incidents of "horseplay" resulting in injury
- Possession of a weapon or a facsimile of one
- Throwing objects, resulting in injury
- Possession or use of a controlled substance
- Sexual, racial, ethnic, or religious harassment
- Abusive, obscene, profane, or disrespectful language or gestures
- Insubordinate refusal to follow a reasonable directive or request
- Theft or vandalism
- General behaviors that are clearly detrimental to the welfare, safety, or morals of the students in the school

Records of Level 2 offenses are kept in a database by infraction, and a discipline file is created for students involved in such incidents. The file includes a record of infractions by year, written and telephone communications with parents, suspension letters, and copies of behavior plans as they are developed and amended. Level 2 offenses always involve a parent contact by the teacher and often by school or district administrators as well. Consequences for Level 2 infractions range from detention to in-school or out-of-school suspension.

Level 3 Offenses. These offenses are of such magnitude that suspension or expulsion is mandatory. They involve situations in which students need to be immediately removed from class or separated from fights that have a high likelihood of injury, credible threats against life or of serious bodily injury, and all types of weapons violations.

For Level 3 offenses, parents are always contacted, and documentation (including suspension letters, behavior contracts, and expulsion briefs) is always prepared. Level 3 offenses often involve the local police, and in these situations, the school obtains arrest records. All Level 3 records follow a student from grade to grade and from elementary to middle to high school.

Figure 24.1 summarizes some of the key differences between Level 1, Level 2, and Level 3 infractions. Schools that use effective school-wide management practices often identify very specific behaviors for each of these categories, along with related consequences.

Establishing Procedures and Practices for Potentially Hazardous Events and Locations

Every school has specific locations and events that can be particularly vulnerable in terms of student misbehavior or accidents, including school assemblies, the lunchroom,

Figure 24.1 Characteristics of Three Levels of Discipline			
	Level of Discipline		
Characteristics	**Level 1**	**Level 2**	**Level 3**
Rules and consequences?	Established and carried out by classroom teacher	Established and carried out at the school level	Established and carried out at the school level
Parent contact?	Possible	Yes	Yes
In-school suspension possible?	No	Possible	No
Out-of-school suspension or expulsion possible?	No	Possible	Yes
Note in student file?	Not usually	Yes	Yes
Referred to law enforcement?	No	Possible	Usually

and waiting areas for school buses, among others. School administrators should establish procedures and practices for these situations to help guide students as well as adults who are supervising these areas or events. Figures 24.2, 24.3, and 24.4, for example, include rules and expectations established by one school for crosswalk safety, assemblies and schoolwide programs, and the cafeteria, respectively.

One area that should receive particular attention from school administrators is the playground and other parts of the school grounds. Specific rules and guidelines to promote safe behavior might be established for the following:

- Swings and other play equipment
- Tackle games and other contact sports

- Bicycles (and, at the high school level, cars and motorcycles)
- Parking lots and pick-up/drop-off areas

Figure 24.5 is an example of the rules and safety guidelines that a high school might establish for the parking lot.

Communicating Expectations to Students and Others

One of the important tasks of the safety and discipline committee is to make sure that all students are aware of schoolwide behavior rules and consequences. One straightforward way to do this is to clarify expectations in a student handbook, as shown in Figure 24.6.

In addition to publishing these expectations in a student handbook, try using some of the techniques for reinforcement that follow.

Figure 24.2
Crosswalk Safety

The following crosswalk guidelines were established with the students' safety in mind. Teachers should review these guidelines with their students several times during the first week of school and then again as needed throughout the school year.

Paraeducators or teachers who supervise children at the crosswalk are expected to know and actively enforce these guidelines:

- Walk on the white crosswalks.
- Follow the crossing guard's instructions; be thoughtful and respectful and use appropriate language.
- Wait on the sidewalk, not in the street, until the crossing guard is in the center of the crosswalk area and signals children to cross.
- Bicycles must be walked across the street.
- Walk at the crosswalk only; diagonal crossing is not permitted.
- Walk, do not run.
- If you drop personal property in the street, ask the crossing guard to retrieve it. Do not run after papers, balls, or any other object.

Figure 24.3

Assemblies and Programs: Guidelines for Teachers

Achieving high standards for behavior in a large-group situation requires attention from all teachers. With high expectations from each adult, our students can exhibit behavior we will all be proud of.

Teachers should set the tone for appropriate behavior as they walk their classes to programs. There should be no talking in the hallways or upon entering the gym. Help students to sit "flat" in a group and remain close for direct supervision (e.g., all students sitting with their legs crossed as opposed to some students kneeling or half-kneeling and half-sitting). Discuss with your class the importance of good audience behavior before a performance. Remind students ahead of time that an adult or student standing in the front of the room indicates that the program is beginning.

Clapping is the *only* acceptable expression of appreciation during assemblies or programs (no whistling or yelling is permitted). Students should use the restroom *before* an assembly. After assemblies or programs, we encourage teachers to reinforce expectations by leading their classes in a discussion of the event and student behavior during the performance or assembly.

Figure 24.4

Expectations for Behavior in the Cafeteria

- Practice good manners and courtesy toward others while waiting in the breakfast or lunch line, while using the vending machines, and while sharing tables.

- Show respect toward others in the cafeteria.

- Speak in quiet voices. Shouting or screaming will not be tolerated.

- Avoid situations in which other students are acting inappropriately or showing a lack of courtesy toward others.

- Handle food appropriately; do not deliberately spill or throw food.

- Pick up your own litter; clean any food from the floor; help clean the table, and leave the area as clean as—or cleaner than—it was when you arrived.

Figure 24.5

Parking Lot Rules and Safety Guidelines

The most important point to remember about driving and parking at school is that this is a privilege, not a right. Students who violate the rules or exhibit unsafe behavior may lose this privilege at any time.

- All cars, mopeds, and motorcycles parked on school grounds or on the streets next to the school must be registered with the main office. Students are expected to provide information about the vehicle, including their name, the name of the owner of the vehicle (if different), the color and make of the vehicle, the license number of the vehicle, and evidence that the vehicle is insured.

- Students may not go to their vehicles during the school day without prior written approval from the main office.

- Bicycles and mopeds may be chained to the rack provided near the main office. These vehicles should not be chained to other school property or to trees.

- Drivers should enter the parking lot only through the gate marked "Entrance" and leave the parking lot only through the gate marked "Exit."

- Drivers should park in a designated parking space only. They should not park in any other area of the parking lot, even if there seems to be room to park there or it seems reasonable to park there. The parking spaces are located where they are for a reason.

- Some parking spaces are designated for handicapped use only. Drivers should respect those who need these spaces by not parking in them without a special permit.

- Drivers speeding through the parking lot, driving in an unsafe manner, deliberately squealing their tires, unnecessarily revving their engines, or violating any of the rules outlined here may be subject to the consequences outlined in the student handbook.

As with all other school rules, you may disagree with these rules, but you may not disrespect or violate them. If you have a suggestion or a specific complaint, please submit a brief, respectful, signed letter (with your name clearly printed as well) to the main office.

Figure 24.6

Sample Handbook Entry for Behavior Expectations

One of the keys to a positive school experience is a discipline structure that helps students learn to behave responsibly. The emphasis at West Elementary School is on maintaining an atmosphere of *mutual respect* that supports learning, working, and achieving. Behavior at school is to be guided by concern for the *safety of children and adults* and *mutual respect for the rights of others.* Through the combined effort of students, their parents or guardians, and the staff, students will develop personal qualities that will benefit them throughout life.

This school has established four broad rules. Children and adults are expected to follow these rules at all times on school grounds:
* Come to school with the goal of learning and producing high-quality work.
* Show courtesy and respect to others at all times.
* Show respect for school property and the rights and property of others.
* Maintain a high rate of attendance and arrive on time.

Students have the security of knowing that *when a rule is broken, discipline will be provided and appropriate consequences will occur.* Depending on the nature, seriousness, or frequency of the problem, a student might apologize, miss a recess, correct a mistake, stay after school, replace broken or stolen property, be silent or out of the classroom for a time, lose a privilege, have a parent called, or receive a suspension.

Fighting, assaults, and other forms of physical aggression are not allowed and will result in one or more consequences. Involved students may
* Be required to participate in a discussion to determine consequences and next steps.
* Be suspended from recess for three to five days.
* Receive an in-school suspension.
* Participate in a conflict resolution session.
* Receive a warning that a second offense will result in half- or full-day suspension. (Depending on the nature of the problem, a student may receive a half- or full-day suspension immediately upon the first offense.)

When establishing consequences, teachers and school officials should be aware of the following:
* Corporal punishment is prohibited by law.
* Students must not be left unsupervised in classrooms during recess because of issues related to safety and personal liability of teachers.
* An entire class of students should not be punished for the poor behavior of a few.
* Sending students outside the classroom for time-out presents a liability issue.

Consistency in behavioral expectations throughout the school helps students understand what is expected of them. Consistent standards should be applied to behavior in classrooms and to conduct in the hallways, the cafeteria, the gym, the playground, the media center, and all other areas of the school and school grounds.

Posters and Handouts. Posters and handouts are straightforward ways to reinforce schoolwide rules for students.

Items in the School Paper or Newsletter. Articles in the school paper or newsletter are good vehicles for topics that warrant discussion, such as changes in the flow of the parking lot, new playground equipment, or particular safety concerns. Short, bulleted lists in the school paper or newsletter also can serve as quick reminders of the safety rules.

Informational Assemblies. As their name implies, informational assembles go beyond written statements and provide opportunities for discussion about schoolwide rules and consequences. For example, during an informational assembly, administrators might give students opportunities to role-play appropriate and inappropriate behaviors, rule infractions, and "bully-proofing" techniques and problem-solving strategies. Assemblies can be opportunities to invite law enforcement personnel to discuss safety and behavior issues that affect the entire school community.

Classroom Visits. Another way to communicate rules and expectations to groups of students is for administrators to visit classrooms on a regular basis and share general data about discipline and responsibility with students. Such visits provide an excellent opportunity for students both to receive positive feedback and to be reminded of school rules and expectations for behavior.

Letters to Parents. One of the most powerful tools a safety and discipline committee has at its disposal is a simple letter to parents. Figure 24.7 shows a letter used by one elementary school to inform parents and guardians about schoolwide rules and expectations for student behavior.

Figure 24.7

Sample Letter to Parents from the Principal

Dear Parents and Guardians,

As the school year begins, I want to take this opportunity to review the rules and guidelines for student behavior that we have established at West Elementary School. We appreciate your support and partnership in reinforcing these expectations with students. Together, we can help ensure that the environment at West Elementary School is safe, healthy, and conducive to effective learning for everyone.

Enclosed is an excerpt from the student handbook regarding schoolwide rules, procedures, and consequences. Please take a few minutes to review these with your child at the beginning of the school year and periodically throughout the school year. The safety and well-being of our students is our highest priority.

Should you have any questions, please don't hesitate to contact me.

Developing a System to Track Behavioral Issues in the School

Unless a school keeps track of behavioral issues, it has no data-driven way to determine if its management techniques at the school level and in individual classrooms are effective. A rigorous tracking system also helps identify students who are prone to extreme behavior and violence. One of the best things a school can do for these students is to develop a system of identifying them as quickly as possible and providing them with the necessary help and support to get their behavior under control. This task is much easier if a school has identified very specific categories of misbehavior. Figure 24.8 shows a sample report for 5th grade

		Figure 24.8		
		Sample Chart for Behavioral Referrals		
Student Name, Initials, or Number	**Date**	**Teacher**	**Specifics**	**Consequences**
JSW	09/28/04	Haystead	Pushing	No lunch recess
WAL	09/29/04	Becker	Hitting on the bus	3-day bus suspension
MJR	09/30/04	Rose	Horseplay	One-week service with Mr. James
MRA	10/06/04	Becker	Hitting	Verbal warning
MRA	10/08/04	Haystead	Hitting	Parents contacted
WAL	10/12/04	Rose	Theft	In-school suspension—1 1/2 days
REB	10/14/04	Haystead	Fighting	Sent home from school
HPI	10/15/04	Waters	Defiant behavior	In-school suspension—half-day
KEF	10/19/04	McRulty	Pushing	No lunch recess—2 days
MRA	10/29/04	Swift	Fighting	In-school suspension—half-day
MRA	11/04/04	Swift	Fighting	Out-of-school suspension—1 day
GJN	11/05/04	Haystead	Hitting	In-school suspension—half-day
KSG	11/09/04	Haystead	Defiant behavior	No specials Friday 11/12
KDC	11/16/04	Waters	Theft	Wrote letter to Mrs. Johnson

students, compiled by the school secretary from daily referrals over several weeks.

It is the job of the safety and discipline committee to analyze the information in these reports. For example, based on reports like this, the committee might conclude that the major behavioral problem in the 5th grade is hitting.

Because the report shown in Figure 24.8 includes students' initials, the school also can identify students who exhibit ongoing problems. To illustrate, consider Figure 24.9, which shows the referrals for one student over four weeks. Based on these data, administrators might decide that this student needs some further assistance, support, and intervention regarding his behavior—and take appropriate action to intervene with the student and ward off future problems.

Figure 24.9 Sample Behavior Report on an Individual Student				
Student Name, Initials, or Number	**Date**	**Teacher**	**Specifics**	**Consequences**
MRA	10/06/04	Becker	Hitting	Verbal warning
MRA	10/08/04	Haystead	Hitting	Parents contacted
MRA	10/29/04	Swift	Fighting	In-school suspension—half-day
MRA	11/04/04	Swift	Fighting	Out-of-school suspension—1 day

Establishing Norms of Conduct for Faculty and Staff

A potential for conflict and discord exists any time a group of people work together, whether they are school-age children or adults. It is all too human to become tired, irritable, and frustrated during times of stress; these emotions can create the conditions for conflict. Realizing this possibility, the safety and discipline committee, along with the principal, can establish norms for behavior among the staff. Such norms not only provide a structure within which faculty and staff can maximize their efficiency, but they also send a strong message to students and parents. If norms of conduct are appropriate to guide the professional behavior of educators, they are also appropriate to guide the behavior of students and parents.

Recommendations for Organizational Practice

In this module, we consider five areas for which norms of conduct might be established:

- How staff will resolve conflicts
- How staff will resolve professional problems and disagreements
- How staff will share information about students

- How staff will share information about one another
- How staff will make decisions

All of these areas can be addressed or revisited in a single activity. For example, teachers meet as an entire faculty, and the areas are listed separately on chart paper and posted around the room. Teachers divide themselves equally around each of the charts and brainstorm strategies and suggestions for each area. They spend five minutes at each chart, writing their strategies and suggestions on it, and moving on cue so that each teacher has had a chance for personal input on each chart.

Teachers are then given one colored dot per chart; as they revisit each chart, they place a dot on the strategy or suggestion that they feel is the most professional way to deal with the issue or norm shown on the chart. Suggestions that have the most dots become the norms and strategies teachers will use to resolve conflicts, address professional disagreements, share information about students, and make decisions. These norms are printed in poster form and are placed in each teacher's office, the main office, and the teachers' lounge.

The school staff can reconsider these norms at the beginning of each year in the same fashion. Teachers place dots on the norms that they wish to keep, and the entire staff is asked for a consensus agreement to follow those norms faithfully for the coming year.

How Staff Will Resolve Conflicts

Conflict resolution is crucial for staff morale. It is widely recognized that unresolved issues between and among staff members can undermine all aspects of organizational effectiveness. Curriculum alignment, goals and feedback, parent communications, school safety, and collegiality and professionalism can all be affected when teachers put personal interests and issues before organizational ones.

For many reasons, the principal has a compelling interest in ensuring that a system of speedy conflict resolution is in place. One effective way to do this is to provide a place or space where staff can "have it out" without fear of administrative reprisal. Faculty and staff at an elementary school in Colorado, for example, know that the principal's office is a safe place for discussing and resolving conflicts with colleagues; when a conflict arises, everyone knows that the principal is available to listen and act as a facilitator of the conversation, not a referee. Participants are assured that anything said in that setting will neither be repeated outside the principal's office nor reflected on anyone's evaluation. In return for adhering to this norm, staff are allowed to openly discuss interpersonal issues in a professional manner without fear of reprisal. Staff members who air personal differences outside of this setting are subject to disciplinary action that can include suspension from school for up to five days without pay.

Another effective norm for resolving conflicts is to agree to "go to the source." This mechanism encourages teachers to meet with each other directly over conflicts and work out solutions together. What is not allowed is the use of e-mail or anything other than direct face-to-face contact in this effort. Teachers who are unable to resolve their differences in this manner are directed to meet with the principal, who acts as facilitator. One of the benefits of this norm is that it helps eliminate the unproductive behavior of complaining about someone to someone else. Some of the unintended consequences of such complaining are that someone's reputation may be damaged, others may unfairly view someone in a poor light, and the person has no opportunity to offer his or her point of view about the situation.

How Staff Will Resolve Professional Problems and Disagreements

Professional problems can quickly degrade into personal ones. Disagreements about teaching style, methodology, philosophy, and management are always present within an organization. The first level of resolution for issues such as these should rest with the teaching team itself. If teachers criticize non–team members, the principal may need to become involved. One way to head off these disagreements is to use faculty meetings as a forum to discuss research and practice by allowing teachers to demonstrate lessons and methods to the faculty as a whole. Another approach is to involve representative teachers in a collaborative process to design a staff development plan that captures common agreements about effective teaching and learning.

How Staff Will Share Information About Students

This area is fairly well governed by the Family Educational Rights and Privacy Act (FERPA) on the one hand and professional discretion on the other. Staff should be made aware of and refreshed on FERPA requirements every year. Beyond that, a portion of time at a staff meeting should be devoted to discussions about parent conference formats, reporting discipline situations to parents, and engaging in "lounge talk." Many schools adopt the norm that teacher-to-teacher conversations about specific student situations should be conducted on a "need-to-know" basis only and that unprofessional gossip should have a well-understood administrative consequence.

How Staff Will Share Information About One Another

The same "need-to-know" requirement is true when staff share information about a colleague on staff with a third party. Staff members should not seek information about their colleagues from a third party unless there is an important reason to do so. Aside from slander and libel laws, there should be well-communicated consequences for staff members who violate personal and professional confidences.

In general, staff should be asked to follow the rule that when they share information about other staff members, they should err on the side of caution, confidentiality, and professionalism. To emphasize this idea, some schools have used quotes that are posted on faculty lounge walls. One such quote, employed at a middle school, was used in a speech by Eleanor Roosevelt but attributed to an unknown author: "Great minds discuss ideas. Average minds discuss events. Small minds discuss people." Similar quotes include

- "Gossip needn't be false to be evil" (Frank A. Clark).
- "Don't repeat anything you wouldn't sign your name to" (Anonymous).
- "There is so much good about the worst of us and so much bad in the best of us, that it ill-behaves any of us to find fault with the rest of us" (James Trulow Adams).

In short, the golden rule of "Do unto others as you would have them do unto you" should apply.

How Staff Will Make Decisions

This area requires quite a bit of discussion and rationale. When staff ask who had the authority to make a decision, frequently they are actually asking, "Why wasn't I involved?" One way to minimize upsets and controversy about the decision-making process is to ensure that everyone clearly understands how staff input will be used and the extent to which it will be considered. For example, at times staff input is collected *in order* to reach a decision (for example, on curriculum materials, the master schedule, budget, staffing). At other times, staff input is sought simply to give people a chance to respond and ask questions. In either case, administrators should ensure that everyone understands the purpose of their input. This approach will help avoid misunderstandings and help build buy-in.

In general, those who are likely to be the most affected by an upcoming decision should be given the greatest opportunity for input (for example, in situations involving hiring, team/grade-level changes, and teaching assignments). However, there are some decisions that only the principal should make (such as those related to reduction in force, nonrenewal, class size, or suspension). The school's approach to various issues should be communicated to staff at the beginning of the year in a meeting or set of meetings whose purpose is to reconfirm how the organization will do business with itself during the upcoming year. In addition, it is good practice to periodically revisit the norms and decisions about the "business of the business" as the year progresses—for example, quarterly.

■ Section Reflection

Checking Your Understanding

Use the space provided to write your answers to the questions.

• You attended a conference during which one of the presenters discussed sta-tistics about school violence and discipline problems, primarily in urban set-tings. You live and work in a rural area; enrollment at your school is very small, and class size is small as well. Other teachers don't see the need for school-level rules and consequences. What is your response?

• Your principal asks you what you think about establishing a committee to deal with school-level safety and discipline issues. Specifically, she wants your suggestions about specific issues the committee or team should address. What is your response?

• You are a member of the safety and discipline committee. In reviewing reports about schoolwide accidents and incidents, you notice that there are a high number of injuries on the new playground equipment compared with previous years. How might you deal with this information?

- Two students are involved in an altercation during lunch. One student now has a black eye. What information do you think should be gathered to determine the appropriate course of action?

- In spite of norms of conduct set at your school, in the faculty lounge you overhear one teacher personally criticizing another teacher. What do you do?

- You disagree strongly with how a teacher is handling discipline issues in his classroom. How do you handle this?

A Self-Assessment

Circle the number on the scale that best matches your situation, with 0 indicating "Not at all" and 4 indicating "To a great extent."

Our school has established an effective hierarchy of discipline.

Our school has established an effective safety and discipline committee or group.

I demonstrate my support for decisions made by my school's safety and discipline team.

I actively communicate school-level discipline procedures to my students.

Our school has established effective norms of staff conduct.

I have contributed to the creation of norms for resolving conflicts, solving professional problems, making decisions, and sharing information about students and staff members.

I have made a commitment to adhere to norms of conduct for faculty and staff at my school.

References

Alberti, R. (1983). *Your perfect right: A guide to assertive living.* San Luis Obispo, CA: Impact.

American Psychiatric Association. (2000). *Diagnostic and statistical manual of mental disorders* (text revision). Washington, DC: Author.

Curwin, R. L., & Mendler, A. N. (1988). *Discipline with dignity.* Alexandria, VA: Association for Supervision and Curriculum Development.

Darwin, C. (1872). *The expression of the emotions in man and animals.* London: John Murray. Available: http://pages.britishlibrary.net/charles.darwin3/expression/expression_intro.htm.

Emde, J. (1991). *Marital communication and stress.* Dissertation, University of Denver, Denver, CO.

Good, T. L. (1987, July–August). Two decades of research on teacher expectations: Findings and future directions. *Journal of Teacher Education, 38*(4), 32–47.

Good, T. L., & Brophy, J. E. (2003). *Looking in classrooms* (9th ed.). Boston: Allyn & Bacon.

Gottman, J., Notarius, C., Gonso, J., & Markman, H. (1976). *A couple's guide to communication.* Champaign, IL: Research Press.

Hunter, M. (1969). *Teach more—faster!* El Segundo, CA: TIP Publications.

Kounin, J. (1970). *Discipline and group management in classrooms.* New York: Holt, Rinehart, & Winston.

Langer, E. J. (1989). *Mindfulness.* Reading, MA: Addison-Wesley.

Lee, F. (1993, April). Disrespect rules. *The New York Times Educational Supplement,* 16.

Marzano, R. J. (1998). *A theory-based meta-analysis of research on instruction.* Aurora, CO: Mid-continent Research for Education and Learning.

Marzano, R. J. (with Marzano, J. S., & Pickering, D. J.). (2003). *Classroom management that works: Research-based strategies for every teacher.* Alexandria, VA: Association for Supervision and Curriculum Development.

Marzano, R. J., Norford, J. S., Paynter, D. E., Pickering, D. J., & Gaddy, B. B. (2001). *A handbook for classroom instruction that works.* Alexandria, VA: Association for Supervision and Curriculum Development.

Marzano, R. J., Pickering, D. J., & Pollock, J. E. (2001). *Classroom instruction that works: Research-based strategies for increasing student achievement.* Alexandria, VA: Association for Supervision and Curriculum Development.

Nansel, T. R., Overpeck, M., Pilla, R. S., Ruan, W. J., Simons-Morton, B., & Scheidt, P. (2001). Bullying behaviors among U.S. youth: Prevalence and association with psychosocial adjustment. *Journal of the American Medical Association 285*(16), 2094–2100.

Notarius, C., & Markman, H. (1993). *We can work it out: Making sense of marital conflict.* New York: G. P. Putnam's Sons.

Nowicki, S., & Duke, M. (1992). *Helping the child who doesn't fit in.* Atlanta, GA: Peachtree.

Pinker, S. (1997). *How the mind works.* New York: W. W. Norton & Company.

Rowland, A. S., Umbach, D. M., Stallone, L., Naftel, A. J., Bohlig, E. M., & Sandler, D. P. (2002). Prevalence of medication treatment for attention deficient-hyperactivity disorder among elementary school children in Johnston County, North Carolina. *American Journal of Public Health* 92(2), 231–234.

Seligman, M. (1990). *Learned optimism*. New York: Pocket Books, Simon & Schuster.

Sieburg, E. (1972). *Toward a theory of interpersonal confirmation*. Internal report. Denver, CO: University of Denver, Department of Communications.

Smith, M. (1975). *When I say no, I feel guilty*. New York: Bantam Books.

Weatherford, V. (1985). An exploratory study of perceived and observed confirmation/disconfirmation communication behaviors in marital dyads. *Dissertation Abstracts International*. (University Microforms No. AAG8517943)

Wubbels, T., Brekelmans, M., van Tartwijk, J., & Admiral, W. (1999). Interpersonal relationships between teachers and students in the classroom. In H. C. Waxman & H. J. Walberg (Eds.), *New directions for teaching practice and research* (pp. 151–170). Berkeley, CA: McCutchan.

INDEX

Page references for figures are indicated with an *f*.

About the Authors

Robert J. Marzano is a Senior Scholar at Mid-continent Research for Education and Learning in Aurora, Colorado; an Associate Professor at Cardinal Stritch University in Milwaukee, Wisconsin; Vice President of Pathfinder Education Inc.; and President of Marzano & Associates. He has developed programs and practices used in K–12 classrooms that translate current research and theory in cognition into instructional methods. An internationally known trainer and speaker, Marzano has authored more than 20 books and 150 articles and chapters on topics such as reading and writing instruction, thinking skills, school effectiveness, restructuring, assessment, cognition, and standards implementation. Recent ASCD titles include *School Leadership That Works: From Research to Results* (2005); *Building Background Knowledge for Academic Achievement* (2004); *Classroom Management That Works: Research-Based Strategies for Every Teacher* (2003); *What Works in Schools: Translating Research into Action* (2003); and *Classroom Instruction That Works: Research Strategies for Increasing Student Achievement* (2001). Marzano received a BA in English from Iona College in New York, an MEd in Reading/Language Arts from Seattle University, and a PhD in Curriculum and Instruction from the University of Washington. Address: 7127 S. Danube Court, Centennial, CO 80016. Telephone: 303-796-7683. E-mail: robertjmarzano@aol.com.

Barbara B. Gaddy is a private consultant and project manager in the field of education. For nearly eight years, she worked at Mid-continent Research for Education and Learning (McREL), serving as Senior Associate and, later, Managing Editor for REL Publications. Prior to joining the McREL staff, she served as Director of Development Communications at the University of Denver. Gaddy co-authored the ASCD publications *Classroom Management That Works: Facilitator's Guide* (Marzano, Gaddy, & D'Arcangelo, 2004) and *A Handbook for Classroom Instruction That Works* (Marzano, Norford, Paynter, Pickering, & Gaddy, 2001). Her other publication credits include *Essential Knowledge: The Debate Over What American Students Should Know* (1999) and *School Wars: Resolving Our Conflicts over Religion and Values* (1996). She earned a BS in Marketing Management from Miami University in Oxford, Ohio, and an MA in Mass Communications and Journalism from the University of Denver. Address: 749 South Vine Street, Denver, CO 80209. Telephone: 303-378-8586. E-mail: barbgaddy@comcast.net.

Maria C. Foseid is a private consultant working with schools and districts throughout the United States. During more than 30 years in education, she has served as Staff Development Coordinator for Cherry Creek School District in Englewood, Colorado; a trainer for Mid-continent Research for Education and Learning; a middle school staff development specialist; and a classroom teacher. Foseid's work centers on the study of learning with practical application of the theory and practice supporting student achievement in a standards-based system. She was a member of the Dimensions of Learning consortium and has done extensive training in Dimensions with teachers and administrators in grades K–12. Foseid has also consulted educators in application of *Classroom Instruction That Works* (Marzano, Pickering, & Pollock, 2001) and on the topics of learning supervision, standards-based education, performance assessment, and reading and writing across the curriculum. She received her BA in English Education and MEd in Curriculum and Instruction from the University of Wisconsin. She completed an educational administration program at the University of Colorado and graduated from the 2001 National Staff Development Academy.

Mark P. Foseid is a private consultant working with schools and districts throughout the country. During more than 30 years in K–12 education, he was an elementary and middle school teacher in all core subject areas, as well as a dean of students, assistant principal, and elementary principal. He has an advanced degree in administration, curriculum, and supervision, and his work centers on the study of learning, with practical applications of the research and strategies supporting student achievement in standards-based systems. Foseid also has consulted educators in the Dimensions of Learning and What Works in Schools programs, standards-based curriculum design, and leadership and organizational development. He received a BS in Biology and Chemistry from the University of Wisconsin and completed a master's program at the University of Colorado. He has industry laboratory research experience and has been recognized by both the Cherry Creek School District and the Colorado Department of Education for excellence in teaching.

Jana S. Marzano has been a psychotherapist in private practice in Colorado for more than 25 years. She is a Licensed Professional Counselor (LPC) and has a master's degree in professional psychology from the University of Northern Colorado in Greeley, Colorado, and a Bachelor of Science in Mental Health Services from Metropolitan State University in Denver, Colorado. She is the co-author of *Classroom Management That Works: Research-Based Strategies for Every Teacher* (2003) and a co-author of a book on vocabulary instruction published by the International Reading Association. Additionally, she has published a number of articles on topics ranging from classroom management to the role of the self-system in determining human behavior. Her areas of specialty include post-traumatic stress disorders, mood disorders, marital counseling, and substance and behavioral addictions. She works extensively with children and adolescents on a variety of issues. Address: 7127 S. Danube Court, Centennial, CO 80016. Telephone: 303-220-1151. E-mail: janamarzan@aol.com.

Related ASCD Resources: Classroom Management

At the time of publication, the following ASCD resources were available; for the most up-to-date information about ASCD resources, go to www.ascd.org. ASCD stock numbers are noted in parentheses.

Audiotapes

Applying Brain Stress Research to Classroom Management (4 live seminars on tape) by Robert Sylwester (#297188)

Conscious Classroom Management: Bringing Out the Best in Students and Teachers by Rick Smith (#202248)

Effective Discipline: Getting Beyond Rewards and Punishment (3 live seminars on tape) by Marvin Marshall (#297190)

Insights on Better Classroom Management from Brain Research by Eric Jensen (#299194)

Proactively Addressing Behavior and Discipline in an Urban Middle School: Implications and Findings by Shelley Beech, Hank Edmonson, Nancy Hale, and Donna Wickham (#201183)

A Timely Approach to Using Proven Strategies for Dealing with Difficult Classroom Behaviors by Louise Griffith and Patricia Voss (#200075)

Using Data to Shape Classroom Practice by Richard DuFour (#299311)

Multimedia

Classroom Management/Positive School Climate Topic Pack (#198219)

Classroom Management Professional Inquiry Kit by Robert Hanson (8 activity folders and a videotape) (#998059)

Dimensions of Learning Complete Program (teacher's and trainer's manuals, book, 6 videos, and an additional free video) Educational consultants: Robert J. Marzano and Debra J. Pickering (#614239)

Networks

Visit the ASCD Web site (www.ascd.org) and search for "networks" for information about professional educators who have formed groups around topics like "Dimensions of Learning" and "Instructional Supervision." Look in the "Network Directory" for current facilitators' addresses and phone numbers.

Online Resources

Visit ASCD's Web site (www.ascd.org) for the following professional development opportunities:

Online Tutorial: *Classroom Management* (free)
Professional Development Online: *Classroom Management: Building Relationships for Better Learning and Dimensions of Learning,* among others (for a small fee; password protected)

Print Products

Beyond Discipline: From Compliance to Community by Alfie Kohn (#196075)

Classroom Management That Works: Research-Based Strategies for Every Teacher by Robert J. Marzano, with Jana S. Marzano and Debra J. Pickering (#103027)

Discipline with Dignity by Richard L. Curwin and Allen N. Mendler (#199235)

Educating Oppositional and Defiant Children by Philip S. Hall and Nancy D. Hall (#103053)

Guiding School Improvement with Action Research by Richard Sagor (#100047)

Key Elements of Classroom Management: Managing Time and Space, Student Behavior, and Instructional Strategies by Joyce McLeod, Jan Fisher, and Ginny Hoover (#103008)

The Results Fieldbook: Practical Strategies from Dramatically Improved Schools by Mike Schmoker (#101001)

What Works in Schools: Translating Research into Action by Robert J. Marzano (#102271)

Videos

How to Design Classroom Management to Enhance Learning (Tape 16 of How To Series) (#403114)

Managing Today's Classroom (3 videos with facilitator's guide) Educational consultant: Rheta DeVries (#498027)

What Works in Schools Video Series (3 videos) Educational consultant: Robert J. Marzano (#403047)

For more information, visit us on the World Wide Web (http://www.ascd.org), send an e-mail message to member@ascd.org, call the ASCD Service Center (1-800-933-ASCD or 703-578-9600, then press 2), send a fax to 703-575-5400, or write to Information Services, ASCD, 1703 N. Beauregard St., Alexandria, VA 22311-1714 USA.